KEPT BY THE POWER

by
Bishop Allen B. Coleman

Kept by the Power
Copyright © 2004 by Bishop Allen B. Coleman

Duplication of any portion of these materials without the express and written consent of the authors is prohibited.

Unless otherwise noted, all quotations are from The King James Version of the Bible.

How to Contact the Author:

Bishop Allen B. Coleman
C/o Voice of Joy Ministries, International
13291-107 Vantage Way
Jacksonville, FL 32218
(904) 741-0506
e-mail: ecc@eccsaints.org

or

5340 Baltimore Ave.
Hyattsville, Maryland 20781

Creative and publishing services by:

CSN Books Publishing
1975 Janich Ranch Court
El Cajon, CA 92019
Toll free: 1-866-484-6184
www.CSNbooks.com

TABLE OF CONTENTS

ACKNOWLEDGMENTS v
TO MY HUSBAND ix

CHAPTER ONE 1
  Everything God Has for You Is Already Yours!

CHAPTER TWO 7
  The Devil Cannot Touch Your Inheritance

CHAPTER THREE 15
  Only A.S.K.: Your Personal Circumstances
  Do Not Matter!

CHAPTER FOUR 19
  You Are Kept by the Power

CHAPTER FIVE 23
  My Relationship With Erik
  Was Kept by the Power!

CHAPTER SIX 31
  Your Lively Hope: Your Inheritance

CHAPTER SEVEN 45
  The Blessings of Renewal

CHAPTER EIGHT 63
  Restoration: Servicing Areas We Don't See

CHAPTER NINE 77
   Redemption: Redeeming What You've Lost

CHAPTER TEN 87
   Keeping Me From Every Evil Work

CHAPTER ELEVEN 99
   The Inheritance That Awaits You

CHAPTER TWELVE 113
   Trained for Your Inheritance

CHAPTER THIRTEEN 129
   The Power of an Heir

BIOGRAPHICAL INFORMATION . . . .

Acknowledgments

As I reflect on the process of stepping out of the boat with this project, I would like to extend special thanks to those who have labored with me. They all truly deserve the credit for turning this dream into an accomplishment.

To my wife, Angela, for all your love and support. Ann, through every journey, with every step, you have always walked hand-in-hand with me. Thank you for your wisdom, insight and your encouragement. You have always reassured me that your love was steady, your support unwavering. Eternity may not be long enough to give you all my love.

To my loving kids (oops, I called you "kids" again!), to Erik, Mary, Erica and Charity. You have encouraged me more than you will ever know. The faith I tried to impart to you has now come back to bless me through your God-filled lives. Thank you.

To my wonderful grandkids, Lamaine, Hannah, Yasmine, and the "new arrival." You guys are Grandpa's heart; you have given me hours of enjoyment, and many principles to preach. I love you!

To my family-my parents, Oscar Coleman, Sr. and Bessie Coleman, and my siblings, whose immeasurable love and encouragement has always enabled me to stand firm in the midst of the storm.

To the Covenant Partners of the "Company of the Faithful," otherwise known as Voice of Joy Ministries Church. From the humblest beginning to the present day, we have pursued, overtaken, and will continue to recover all.

To Vanilla Pittman, Andrea Selby, Barbara Terrell, and Cynthia Glover (and your families) for your untiring support and undying loyalty. You are truly bondservants in the Kingdom, and your worth is too valuable to measure. You all make me better than what I am and you help me to multiply the value of "Whose I am."

To my "Friend of a Friend," Apostle Michael and Pastor Arline Fields of Lumberton, NC. Man, you all have been loyal friends, trusted advisors, and steadfast counselors. As iron, you have sharpened me time and time again; my countenance has been made better for it.

To my trusted friends and travel partners, Pastors Ken and Charlene Williams. You all have epitomized unconditional love and service, true friendship, and genuine relationship. Ken, you have selflessly made me shine on both ends of the world; I deeply love and appreciate you for your sacrifice. Thanks.

To Mike, Tim and Terri Wourms, and the powerfully gifted CSN family—you folks are truly awesome! Thanks for holding my hand through uncharted waters.

To Shirley Baker and Vivian Seymour, whose gentle prodding has been a source of motivation for me through the years. Ladies, you didn't give up; you kept speaking it. The gate is open now, and I'll never allow it to close.

Last, but most assuredly not least—to my Lord and Savior, Jesus Christ. Thank You for being my total

Source of life and inspiration. You have truly kept me by Your power and daily You give me new reasons to fall in love with You.

Lord, I forever say Yes!

Bishop Allen B. Coleman

To My Husband

Allen,

Thank you for not giving up on your dream. Though there were many obstacles, you still pressed on knowing that this book is only the beginning of many more to come. There are so many completed books inside of you, and I will be right there assisting you in bringing them all to pass.

May this book be an example of how we have been *Kept By the Power* for nearly three decades now. God's keeping power has been our standard of living, and continues to be so in the lives of our children, our grandchildren, and to the many spiritual sons and daughters the Lord has privileged us to parent.

Thank you for being all that you are to me, our family, our church, and most of all, to our Heavenly Father. It was your intense love for the Lord that drew me close to you.

We love you so very much.
Your Wife and Lifetime Partner,
Angela

CHAPTER ONE

Everything God Has for You Is Already Yours!

One of the most powerful revelations you will find in Scripture is this amazing truth:

Everything that God has for you is already yours!

Imagine...

You do not need to do anything more to receive His blessings! Once you accept Jesus into your life, you cannot be "more saved." Once you receive the righteousness of God, you cannot become "more righteous."

So many Christians are wasting their energy trying to figure out ways to make us more saved and more right, but there are no new ways to do that. You see, once you have received God by faith, you are already everything He needs you to be. In fact, one definition of righteousness is "to be in Christ, all that God requires you to be, and all you could never be within yourself."

Life is not about your Monday mornings, and your

good days or your bad days. Your right days will never outweigh your not-so-right days because when you receive Him, His blood covers everything!

Bury the Past

A brother once said to me, "But Allen, remember the time when you did so and so?"

"Well, if I wanted to make myself remember, I could," I replied. "But all I remember right now is that my old carcass named 'Allen' went to a cemetery called the 'past.' I buried him in a graveyard called 'ambition' and walked away, refusing to cry. I stepped away, rejoicing as I closed and locked that cemetery gate. I will never go back there again because the past is past."

That attitude is not some "feel good" philosophy to conceal my guilt from my past sins! It is a Biblical attitude birthed out of God's own heart.

As far as the east is from the west, so far hath he removed our transgressions from us.
(Psalm 103:12)

You may have been a liar, a cheater, or a deceiver, but when you pass through the blood of Jesus, there is no memory and no remembrance of what you once were!

If anybody tries to remind you of what you were, tell them, "I beg your pardon, I don't know who you are talking about. I was there on the day they printed the obituary; I was there when that old man died. Now my life is hidden with Christ in God, and everything old about me is dead; everything about Him is now alive in me."

Chapter One: Everything God Has for You

MAGNIFIED IN HIM

From the first day of your new life in Christ, to this present time, He is making you more and more like Him. If you put a magnifying glass over a butterfly, does the butterfly become bigger? David said in Psalm 34:3, "Oh, magnify the Lord with me." Notice, God will not get any bigger, but the perfection of Him in you will grow.

From the first day of your salvation to the present day, God wants you to keep looking to Him, to keep allowing Him to be magnified in you so that He keeps getting bigger.

The bigger He becomes in you, the more benefit you reap from Him.

Every day of your life you are dead, but you are alive in Him.

BORN INTO AN INCREDIBLE INHERITANCE

My positional Scripture for this book revolves around 1 Peter.

> *Peter, an apostle of Jesus Christ, to the strangers scattered throughout Pontus, Galatia, Cappadocia, Asia, and Bithynia, elect according to the foreknowledge of God the Father, through sanctification of the Spirit, unto obedience and the sprinkling of the blood of Jesus Christ; grace unto you and peace be multiplied. Blessed be the God and Father our Lord Jesus Christ, which according to His abundant mercy has begotten us again, unto a lively hope, by the resurrection of Jesus Christ from the dead.*
> (1 Peter 1:1-3)

Everything God is doing in you He has already given you. It has been reserved and kept "to an inheritance incorruptible, and undefiled" (verse 4), reserved for you in heaven. Verse 5 further declares that you are one who is "kept by the power of God through faith, unto salvation ready to be revealed in the last times."

The Amplified Bible says it a bit differently, and offers some additional spiritual insight.

> *You are born into an inheritance which is beyond the reach of change and decay, it is imperishable and it is reserved in heaven for you who are being guarded, surrounded by God's power through your faith until you fully inherit that final salvation.*

God has given you the Kingdom–anything and everything that brings you increase!

God has already reserved your inheritance for you in heaven!

When you receive Jesus, you are born of God and become a citizen of heaven.

> *Being born again, not of corruptible seed, but of incorruptible, by the word of God.*
> (1 Peter 1:23)

Literally, right now you are a citizen of heaven, and your blessings come from an account you have in heaven. If you are a child of God, call on Him to receive your abundant inheritance, your spiritual blessings.

Start to pray out loud words such as these:

Chapter One: Everything God Has for You

"Father, I thank You for Your inheritance, and I hereby put a demand on my health, on my wealth, on my peace, on my safety and on my security.

"Thank You, Lord, that all of these things are reserved in heaven for me as my abundant inheritance. Amen."

Your Inheritance is Already in Your Account!

Your inheritance in heaven is incorruptible (verse 4). The Amplified Bible reminds us that "it is beyond the reach of decay." Every blessing God has for you cannot rust or become old, and is already yours in the heavens. The devil cannot take from you something that has already been reserved for you in heaven!

Let me clarify how this works in the spiritual realm by giving an example in the natural realm.

The customer who deposits money with the Bank of America cannot just walk up to the Bank of Wachovia and take out that money.

Why?

Because that person deposited money with the Bank of America, not the Bank of Wachovia. The "Wachovians" have placed their money in the Bank of Wachovia. All day long the "Wachovians" can look into the windows of the Bank of America, but there would be no reason for them to go inside because the Bank of America cannot do anything for them. Oh, they could go in and walk through the nice lobby, but they cannot get in the teller's line because they have nothing deposited in that bank.

The same is true in the spiritual realm: nothing in, nothing out.

But 1 Peter 1:23 says you are born of God, not of a corruptible seed, but of an incorruptible seed, by the Word of God. You are a citizen of heaven, and your blessings come from heaven.

Know where your account is located...in heaven. To receive it, you must go into the bank of the heavenlies. If you are a child of God, you can call on God to receive your blessings.

Chapter Two

The Devil Cannot Touch Your Inheritance

Your blessing is incorruptible, "beyond the reach of decay."

Every blessing God has for you will not grow old. The devil cannot take from you something that has already been reserved in your name.

So many Christians walk in fear, afraid they are going to lose their children, their marriage, their minds or their jobs. How can you lose your job if it comes from God? How can you lose your health if it comes from God?

Your inheritance is beyond the reach of decay, devastation and death!

> *Blessed be the God and Father of our Lord Jesus Christ who has blessed us with all spiritual blessings in heavenly places in Christ.*
>
> (Ephesians 1:3)

All your blessings are in heavenly places! If your blessings are in heavenly places, and you are a child of God, where do you live? In heavenly places.

Stop calling on others to try and receive what you want...call on and receive from God. Jesus said, "Lay up your treasures in heaven" so the moths, the rust, and the decay cannot corrode or destroy it.

Your blessings are not subject to foreclosure or bankruptcy.

You do not need to worry about remembering your security system code. As long as you know that your blessings are in heavenly places, all you need to do is place a demand on the blessings already deposited in your heavenly bank account.

Withdrawals From Your Heavenly Bank

How do you get money out of your heavenly bank account?

Well, for one thing, you do not go in as a beggar, resting your head weakly on the counter, hoping the teller will help you. If you mope in front of her long enough, the teller might say to you, "Sir, I cannot help you until you fill out paper."

"Oh no," you timidly reply, "I knew you were going to make it hard for me."

"Just fill out the paper, sir," the teller says, trying to encourage you. "After you complete the slip, I'll be happy to give you the money."

"Oh, no. Woe is me."

"Sir, please fill out the paper. Don't you want some money today?"

Chapter Two: The Devil Cannot Touch Your Inheritance

"No, this process is just too hard," you reply as you walk away without a single dime.

As silly as that scenario sounds, so many Christians act timidly before God, begging for a crumb here and there.

Stop being so obstinate and stubborn with God!

When you go to your regular bank, all you need to do is write down your name and your account number, and tell them how much money you want. If you do not know your account number, your name will pull up the account number in the computer. Next, you write down the amount you want, and if it is in your account, the bank will give it to you!

It is that simple.

So too with God—He operates the same way.

When He placed health into your heavenly account, He expected you to know your account number, or at least to know that you have an account, so you could withdraw from the heavenly realm.

When He placed prosperity into your heavenly account, He expects you to know that you must present a request for payment to receive your funds.

When He placed peace into your heavenly account, He expects you to know where to go (not the world's bank) to make your withdrawal.

Take No Thought

In Matthew 6:25, we discover that once we start putting ourselves in heaven, our account is there waiting. This verse is the payoff for knowing the location of your account:

Therefore I say unto you, <u>take no thought</u>.

"But Pastor, you don't understand how little I got paid this week."

Take no thought.

"But the team of doctors all said there is no hope for me."

Take no thought.

"You don't understand, I didn't get my overtime check this week."

Take no thought.

My Bible reads, "take no anxious thought." Why? Because there is nothing to worry about if your account is in heaven.

> *Take no thought for your life, what ye shall eat, or what ye shall drink; nor yet for your body, what ye shall put on. Is not the life more than meat, and the body than raiment? Behold the fowls of the air; for they sow not, neither do they reap, nor gather into barns; yet your heavenly Father feedeth them. Are ye not much better than they?*
>
> (Matthew 6:25-26)

The birds do not sow seeds. They do not stand in lines trying to get some cheese. They do not need to be re-certified.

Your Heavenly Father will feed you all you need

Chapter Two: The Devil Cannot Touch Your Inheritance

because you are worth so much more to Him than the birds!

> *Which of you by taking thought can add one cubit to his height? And why should you take thought for your clothing? Consider the lilies of the fields, how they grow. They toil not and neither do they spin. And yet I say unto you, even Solomon and all his glory was not dressed like these lilies. If God so clothed the grass which is here today and gone tomorrow, shall He not much more clothe you? Now, therefore, I say unto you, 'take no thought saying, what are we going to eat? What are we going to drink? Or wear all shall we be clothed.'"*
>
> (Matthew 6:27-31)

Isn't that what your Bible says?

Notice that your Heavenly Father knows that you have need of all these things.

Your Heavenly Account Number

You have an account number!

Matthew 6:33 reveals the account number you need to receive from your heavenly bank account.

> *But seek ye first the kingdom of God and His righteousness, and all these things shall be added unto you.*

What things?

The things you would normally worry about; the things that would normally give you anxious thought.

Clothing.

Gas for your car.

The food to feed your kids.

Rent.

Know your account number. Even if you are on the other side of the world, when you have your heavenly number, help is always on the way. You have a worldwide, heavenly bank.

We understand that our Visa card is good around the world, but sometimes we do not have enough to trust our heavenly bank account on the next block.

Let me tell you a story about my earthly Visa card. Hopefully, it will help you understand the far-reaching nature of your heavenly account.

After a week of intense ministry in India, I decided my last meal in the hotel's restaurant would be daring. "Tonight, I am going spicy," I boldly declared at my table. My travel partner, Pastor Williams, replied, "Bishop, you may not want to do that."

"What are you talking about?" I questioned. "I want to go spicy."

"Bishop, you are in India," he replied, "The spicy food we eat back home is much different than here."

"I'm going spicy," I stubbornly replied. I then told the waiter, "I want the mixed fried rice. Spicy." Backtracking I asked, "Tell me, just how spicy is it?"

"It is not very bad. But perhaps you should order the mild, or the 'little spicy,'" he replied.

Chapter Two: The Devil Cannot Touch Your Inheritance

"O.k.," I replied, "just give me the 'little spicy.'"

Well, you have probably guessed by now what happened. That meal was so spicy that even the smell of it made me break out in a sweat! That smell got up into my left nostril and would not leave. When I put the first forkful of rice in my mouth, I felt like I was on fire!

"Sir, is it good?" the waiter asked.

"Just leave," I tersely replied, trying to catch my breath. That meal was so spicy that I thought it would burn a hole in the table.

This story may seem like a long way around to make my point, but here it is: when I came to the end of my meal, I pulled out my VISA card. "Visa" is not an Indian term, but is recognized and accepted for payment around the world, even on the meal I could not eat. My Visa account was working even though I was 10,000 miles away from home, struggling to breathe. My card operated and was activated to pay for my uneaten meal.

YOUR ETERNAL ACCOUNT AND PIN NUMBER

My Visa account is international.

Your account with God is more than national or international...it is eternal.

Whether your need is from yesterday, today or tomorrow, God says, "If you know the access code, if you know the personal password, if you have the account number, whether you need a small bunch of blessings or a big bunch of blessings, I'm going to pour them out if you have the right account number."

Your account number is Matthew 6:33: <u>seek Him first</u> and all your needs will be added unto you.

> *Take no thought for tomorrow. Tomorrow will take thought for the things of itself.*
>
> (Matthew 6:34)

Each day has enough to worry about without trying to anticipate or worry about the future. I honestly believe that some people get worried just because their lives are going so good that they cannot find anything to worry about.

You have a heavenly PIN (personal identification number) as well, and it is found in Matthew 7:7. Your three-letter PIN number says,

> <u>A</u>*sk, and it will be given to you;* <u>s</u>*eek, and you will find;* <u>k</u>*nock, and it will be opened to you.*

God gives His blessings to the rich and to the poor. We all have the same opportunity; we all have the same password; we all have the same access code:

A (ask) **S** (seek) **K** (knock)

If you ask, you will receive.

"How do I know my heavenly blessing is coming, Bishop?"

"Because 1 Peter promises that it is reserved for you in heaven. Ask and it shall be yours. The only thing that keeps you from receiving is not asking, not using your personal pin number."

Chapter Three

ONLY A.S.K.:
Your Personal Circumstances Do Not Matter!

God's blessings do not depend on any particular set of circumstances.

- You can have curly hair or be bald.
- You can have a great deal of education or none at all.
- You can be black, white or yellow.
- You can have plenty of common sense or not an ounce of it.

Whatever your current state, you were born into your inheritance!

If you ask for it, you will receive it.

The only difference between people who have and the people who do not have is that they know how to ask. Going back to our example with the Bank of America, a rich uncle could deposit $1,000,000 into your account, but until you ask for it, that money will just sit there.

The same is true of your heavenly bank account. God has already made every deposit you will ever need, but until you ASK for it, your heavenly heritage just sits there.

Many Christians spend more time trying to find excuses than they do asking.

If you read through the entire passage in Matthew 7:8 it reads: "For everyone that asks, receives."

Everyone?

Of course. God's promises are for all who love and receive Him.

You can still stubbornly reserve the right to try and find reasons why God's blessings cannot be yours. But here's a Biblical truth: you are an everyone, and all of the "everyones" qualify for the blessings of the Lord.

Some do not have the courage or the confidence to ask. Yet, the blessings are already in place, deposited into your account.

A-S-K is an acronym. A-S-K breaks down to: A for ask, S for seek, and K for knock.

Everyone that asks, seeks, and knocks – receives.

Look for the Demon in Your Own Mirror

The largest demons of all are not found in the horror movies or in the dark places, but in our mirrors. Through poor self-esteem and low self-image, we sometimes beat up ourselves the same way the devil tries to torment us. These "demons" in the mirror tell us many lies.

Chapter Three: Only A.S.K.

"You can't ask, you are too black."
"You can't ask, you are too white."
"You can't ask, you were raised poor."

The Word says that everyone who asks receives.

God does not need to create a blessing to give it to you; it is already created and reserved in heaven for you. The "Wachovians" cannot go storming into the Bank of America because they do not have an account at that bank. But those with Bank of America accounts can walk in like they own the place and expect to receive from the Bank of America because that bank is reserved for them.

Everything you have or will need is reserved for you in your account.

What Does Your Account Contain?

1 Peter 1:4-5 tells what is in your account.

To an inheritance incorruptible, and undefiled, and that fadeth not away, reserved in heaven for you, who are kept by the power of God through faith unto salvation ready to be revealed in the last time.

Your inheritance is incorruptible!

Inflation cannot touch it, depression cannot rob it, hard times cannot erode it.

Your inheritance is undefiled, free from decay!

You may ask, "but what if I'm a backslider, and I have just decided to come back to the Lord. Do I have to start all over again?"

NO! You do not need to start over again. Your account is still there in heaven. And while you were away from the Lord, you did not forfeit one dime of interest! Nothing in it decayed or became corrupt.

Your account still has healing in it, still has wealth in it, still has prosperity in it, still has a sound mind in it.

For God hath not given us the spirit of fear; but of power, and of love, and of a sound mind.
(II Timothy 1:7)

You may not have been at a place to access your account during the years of your backsliding, but it is still your account.

And, on the day you sincerely repent, you can ask for it and it will be released to you.

CHAPTER FOUR

You Are Kept by the Power

Some would say, "Bishop, I am glad my heavenly account is up there for me, but I don't feel good enough and worthy enough to go get it."

Who are kept by the power of God through faith unto salvation ready to be revealed in the last time.

(I Peter 1:5)

This inheritance is reserved in heaven, not because you are worthy, but because you are kept by the power of God!

You do not need to walk in the fear of losing the blessing because you are kept by the power. The Amplified Bible reads that those...

Who are being guarded, surrounded by God's power through your faith. Until that which is in the heavens is enjoyed in the earth.

Your help is in the heavens waiting for you to write out a withdrawal slip.

Your account number is <u>seek first the kingdom of God</u> and His righteousness, and all these things are going to be added to your life.

Your PIN number is: A.S.K.

All you need to do is to place a demand on what is already in your account.

Your Bible is your statement of benefits. He has sent His Word to heal you, to deliver you. He said in Isaiah 53:5:

> *He was wounded for my transgressions, bruised for my iniquities, the chastening of my peace was upon Him, with His stripes I am healed.*

If you are already healed, then your benefits declare that you have a healing. All you need to do is complete a withdrawal slip and furnish your PIN number.

Claim Your Inheritance

Begin to ask, to lay hold of, to stake a claim to your blessings; everyone who asks receives. Whether you are suffering from a common cold, or have a terminal illness, ask and you will receive because you are kept by the power.

Imagine...

Your inheritance is kept in heaven for you.

The word "kept" means "to have a watcher, to mount a guard." You have a guard watching you, looking out

Chapter Four: You Are Kept by the Power

for you. Your pockets may be empty, but you still have an undefiled inheritance waiting that cannot be stolen from you; you cannot lose it.

Rest in peace knowing that you have a treasure in heavenly places.

> *Blessed be the God and Father of our Lord Jesus Christ, who hath blessed us with all spiritual blessings in heavenly places in Christ:*
> (Ephesians 1:3)

Place a demand on it now.

How to Activate the Demand

Let me give you an example of how this principle works.

Recently, a man came to me who had been unemployed in his specific field for six months. He continued to do everything he knew how to do: submitting resumes and doing odd jobs to help support his family."

"The Scripture says that you are blessed with all spiritual blessings *in heavenly places*," I told him, "and your treasure (income) *is laid up in heaven*. So, let's agree together and make a withdrawal today. Let's put a demand on your heavenly account so you can take care of your family.

Things were looking bad.

His wife began to worry.

Her husband told her, "Honey, I have submitted this

entire issue to God. I am already doing the possible. But I actually stand a better chance unemployed in God's hands than I do in my own hands."

After we put a demand on his account, within the thirty days he had received more income than most people make in a year!

Why?

Because His blessings were being kept by God's power, and he submitted his demand. Now, he has the funds to take care of his family.

Are you in the same situation as the gentleman I just described? Are you working two and three jobs just to break even?

Put a demand on your "Kept By The Power" account. Start working as unto the Lord and earn more.

"How is that possible, Bishop?"

You do not have to work eight hours and then stress out in the other sixteen. Rely on your Heavenly Father as your source, and not your job.

God's blessing is kept for you.

Your inheritance is preserved for you.

Chapter Five

My Relationship With Erik Was Kept by the Power!

As I pondered on how to communicate this truth into printed form, I wrestled with the prospect of sharing this very personal example from my own life. I discussed it with my family (numerous times) and through their very wise counsel, I determined that the good that can come from this information will far outweigh any negative backlash.

Everyone has a past, and if sharing a portion of mine further clarifies this powerful revelation, then so be it.

The more I came into the revelation that God is reserving my blessings for me, the more it seemed that God Himself began tugging on my heart and mind, forcing me to face the unresolved issues that plagued me. You see, it is easy to say that you have no problems, that everything is just fine. In reality, we all came to Jesus with a past, and we trust Him daily to give us a better future.

Unrelenting disappointment leaves you heartsick, but a sudden good break can turn life around.
(Proverbs 13:12, The Message Bible)

Each of us must come to terms with the question marks in our lives.

Failed projects, deferred hopes and dreams, and strained relationships.

Prayers that seem to be delayed or unanswered. We wonder, "Will it ever end?"

Yes, it will, and God's Word proves it.

Let them shout for joy, and be glad, that favour my righteous cause; yea, let them say continually, Let the LORD be magnified, which hath pleasure in the prosperity of his servant.
(Psalm 35:27)

It is your Heavenly Father's "righteous cause," His aim or mission, to see that His servants prosper (be fulfilled)!

The more I began to understand this biblical principle, the more I noticed a changing desire to seize fulfillment in my own personal life at a higher level.

The Pain of Pursuing the Promise

As I pursued the promises of God, there seemed to be a mark, a brand of discomfort attached to my pursuit. It may have come from the memory of the struggle of past pursuits; it may have come from projects, journeys or crusades that all began with a wonderful bang and ended dashed on the rocks, ruined.

Regardless, it was there.

As I seemed to move closer to the promise, the pain, the memories, the "heartsickness" would always increase.

This is what some people go through when they have challenges in their marriages. They have such a history of non-fulfillment in their relationship that they have been reduced to legal roommates, and not a couple. The prospect of a love-filled, romantic relationship yielded to a stale, dark life of pain. As long as they have the pain, they will never reach out to experience the full potential of the marriage union.

My Breakthrough With Erik

My oldest child, Erik, is my son from a previous relationship. Erik lived with his mother most of the time, and because of the strain on the relationship, I was unable to see him consistently. After making several attempts to resolve custody and visitation issues, I reasoned that it was too stressful on my son to play tug-of-war with his life. I reluctantly backed away, deciding I couldn't handle the problem.

Shortly thereafter, I became born again. I met and married my beautiful wife, and began a family of our own. Though she knew all about my son, she never stood in the way of my efforts to pursue a relationship with him; she even encouraged it because she knew the incredible pain I harbored. She felt I would never be complete until this relationship issue was resolved.

Years passed. I graduated from Bible college, began traveling extensively, and finally settled down to pastor a church. We saw Erik maybe three times throughout this entire period.

Then, he seemed to vanish from the earth. We didn't know how to reach him, and we assumed that he was not allowed to reach us.

I noticed that during times of prayer, thoughts would come to me about my son, like a prompting, a prodding in my mind to pursue him again. I pushed them away because of the years of drama associated with wanting him to be in my life.

Over time, these thoughts intensified. It became apparent to me that somebody bigger than myself was bringing up the relationship.

What Is Your Erik?

Your unresolved issue may not involve your children. In fact, it may have nothing to do with a strained relationship.

It could be the job where you were falsely accused of some wrongdoing and terminated.

It could be the lingering sickness, or pattern of affliction, that keeps you in physical and financial crisis.

Whatever the area, the Father wants to bring closure to that area.

In my own case, God did just that.

One day my wife came to me and said, "Wow, I just

Chapter Five: My Relationship With Erik

feel like Erik will be around us soon. I don't know how it will happen, but I believe God is working it out."

Though I wanted to be excited about this declaration, I wasn't totally. I was thinking, "If Erik does come back into our lives, what will it be like? What problems will he bring with him? How can we ever catch up on the years that we've missed?"

One day as I was in prayer for one of the other children in the congregation, thoughts of Erik came on me so strongly that I stopped...and this time I yielded.

"OK, Lord, I know it's You; whatever You have for me, however You bring him back, I trust You. I'm tired of hurting, and I'm tired of longing. No matter how he comes–just bring him home. If he comes with fruits, flakes and nuts, it doesn't matter. I want my son, Lord. I want my son."

Everything was still and quiet as a peace came over me. It was evident that I no longer had this weight on my shoulders. I was like a man who had just been exonerated from some huge wrong.

The pain, the strain that had lingered for many years was gone. The ball and chain I pulled around were gone. I didn't know how God was going to heal the relationship, or when I would see Erik, but I knew it was done because God Himself was now working on my case.

A peace came over me.

From then on, when I would pray, it did not come up anymore because I had already handled it with God; I was taking hold of the promise.

Give Him Your Empty Holes

My mother died when I was 9, and her funeral was on my 10th birthday. For years I carried that empty hole inside of me, and had to do the same thing I did with Erik. Every time I'd get ready to pray, God would bring my mother's death up to me until I dealt with it, until I grabbed it.

Then peace came, and it was over.

Now, back to Erik.

November, nothing happened.

December, nothing happened.

At the church, I had just been given the o.k. to start our Bible College, but we were not ready. That year we had some young ladies who heard me announce the college in church, and they generously volunteered to help, even though it was on a holiday weekend.

On Christmas Eve, these ladies came in for four hours to help me organize the Bible College, scheduled to start in the New Year. I was very excited.

When everyone was gone, I went to shut off the lights when the telephone rang...on Christmas Eve!

I let the phone ring until the answering machine almost picked it up. I'm thinking, "Somebody obviously knows I am here." So, I picked up the phone and on the other end I heard "Dad?"

"Dad who?" I thought.

I began to tremble. The "thing" that had been kept for me for all these years — associated with pain, heartache, discouragement and disappointment — was now talking to me on the phone!

But "it" had been *kept by the power* of God for this moment when a new relationship would begin between my son and me!

Every time you get a revelation that God is holding onto your things for you, and you start using your access code and pin number, God will bring up those areas that are still unfinished business in your life.

You may feel the pain and let go, but He will bring it up again until you grab it and do not let go. When I held on to the promise, He brought Erik back to me.

I had experienced so many tormenting thoughts.

"You are mentoring everybody else's child, you're going to raise up sons and daughters all over who will follow the Word, but what about your own son?"

Thankfully, I do not have to answer those self-accusations any more.

HOLD ON TO THE PROMISE

When you hold on to the promise, your answer comes through the door. If you try to chase the problem without the benefit of the promise, you will fail. But, when you receive a revelation, God's Word will always prevail!

I did not know what was going on with Erik when he called. I came to learn that he had experienced some hard times. But whenever he could have made a decision against God, something else happened.

Why?

Because he was being kept by the power.

Friend, you may have a son living far away from home who is all alone; he does not know a single soul. But when you pray and hold onto the promise, you will receive a revelation that God is keeping him for you. When he walks around, doing whatever he wants to do, he has an angel with him. When somebody wants to fight him, the angel is standing in front of him. When somebody wants to shoot him, boom, the angel takes the bullet. With every major thing that could cost him his life, God rescues him, even when you do not know what is going on.

We did not know where Erik was, or if he was alive or dead, but we did know that God was keeping our inheritance safe!

RELEASE THE PAIN – POSSESS THE PROMISE!

I do not care what your pain is, you do not need to live with that pain or regret any longer. When the enemy tries to bring up the past, surrender that thing to God. The enemy will say, "If you just loosen your stand a little bit, you may be all right. You see, with this commitment thing to God, all you are doing is turning people off. You need to loosen up your stand a little bit. Just loosen up."

Tell the enemy, "I am completely kept by the power of God!"

Give up your regrets and pain today, and thank Jesus for His promise.

CHAPTER SIX

Your Lively Hope: Your Inheritance

God has His blessings reserved for you in your heavenly bank account. One young man in our church discovered that truth in a very personal way.

James (not his real name) had fallen away from the things of God. He told me, "In the troubles of my past years, all I could remember were your sermons where you shared the Word. They were in my spirit, floating through me."

Remember our foundational Scripture, 1 Peter 1:3?

> *Blessed be the God and Father of our Lord Jesus Christ, which according to his abundant mercy hath begotten us again unto a lively hope by the resurrection of Jesus Christ from the dead.*

He has birthed in us a lively hope!

You can hang your entire salvation, all your victories and triumphs, all your successes, every smile and all your happiness can hang on that hope.

Your hope came through the resurrection of Jesus Christ from the dead, and that miraculous event has also resurrected you into an inheritance which is incorruptible!

Contrary to what you might think, this inheritance was NOT activated by your salvation. It was ALREADY ACTIVATED before you got saved. It was activated the second Jesus was raised from the dead.

Never let anybody tell you that certain things only happen when you get saved. If you never get saved, heaven is still for you...you just failed to take advantage of your inheritance.

Your inheritance is incorruptible, undefiled and it will not fade away. The Amplified says it is "beyond the reach of decay, it is unsullied and unfaded. It is reserved in heaven for you."

Your inheritance is reserved!

But there's more!

Many preachers will declare that "you are born unto a lively hope," but then they add, "that hope will not come to you until after you have closed your eyes on this side." That is simply not accurate. The Lord's prayer says, "Let your will be done on earth as it is being done in heaven."

What's being done in heaven?

Your inheritance is being held up there. It is not held in heaven to keep it from you, it is held up there to keep it from decay!

Chapter Six: Your Lively Hope: Your Inheritance

GOD IS NEVER LATE WITH BLESSINGS

Heaven is a timely place. Your blessings do not arrive late when you are in heaven...they are right on time. Your blessings are reserved in heaven, and verse 5 tells us that they are *kept by the power* of God through faith unto salvation, ready to be revealed in the last times.

Look at Jude 24, a passage we call the Great Benediction: *Now unto him that is able to keep you.*

Digest each word of that statement.

"Keep" means "to guard you, to put sentinels around you, to set a watcher around you." On your good days, on your bad days, on your right days and on your wrong days, the watcher is still there.

"The Highlander" was an old television program I used to watch. They had a group of people on that show who could not touch things, so they were called "watchers."

Your angel is a watcher, but he can touch things! He can see you are about to get into trouble, and he will try to steer you away from it. He can see you going down Main Street and recognize an impending problem. He can whisper in your ear, "Don't go that way." He can see the two gangs that have decided to wage a turf war just three blocks from where you are about to walk into a drive-by where you will be caught in the crossfire.

You have all had moments like this.

A quiet voice speaks down inside of you, and you just stop. Why? Because God is keeping you.

Continue Your Forward Motion

Now unto him that is able to keep you from falling.

Falling is going back, being deceived, fainting, failing. Falling is anything that stops a forward motion.

God wants to keep you from ever stopping your forward motion!

Now, here's an interesting twist: walking is continuing to fall...with a foundation. When you walk, your foot begins to get firmly planted; your foundation keeps you. But then your foot moves and you are actually falling. Then your foot engages again, without you ever telling it to do so; it is an automatic response.

Who put that response in you?

"Now unto him that is able to keep" that foot engaged to stop you from falling.

Then Why Did I Fall?

Several years ago, I had four of my staff tender their resignations in one month. The previous month, someone had declared that "The winds of change are blowing through."

Now, even if winds are blowing, you still have to choose whether to be affected by them or not. Even having this prophetic warning didn't keep those staff members from falling. It was the lack of being firmly planted *when* the wind came.

It is my job to preach the Word in season and out of

Chapter Six: Your Lively Hope: Your Inheritance

season. As I do, God will keep me. And when others get caught up in a wind, my job is to pray for them, trust the word of the Lord, and believe that those who allow God to keep them *will be kept.*

Because sometimes, that wind could be a wind of deception. When that wind has hit, if you are caught up into it, if it impedes your progress, recognize that there is a problem. God wanted to keep you, but you did not have a forward motion.

Presenting God's Trophy

Now unto him that is able to keep you from falling and to present you.

Have you ever been to a program where they presented a person, almost with the implication that the person is "a trophy"? So, if I present my child as an honor roll student, I am trying to exhibit a model of academic power. If I present you, like Jude says, as "faultless," then I am trying to show that you are a trophy.

You are God's trophy in a world that is full of sin, hell, and damnation; He shows you as faultless.

When you could fall, you don't fall.

When you could fail, you don't fail.

When you could go back, you don't go back.

When you could be sick, you're not sick.

When you could be broke, you're not broke.

When you could be losing, you're not losing.

God said, "I am presenting you."

"Well, God, who are you presenting me to?"

The world, the flesh, and the devil.

God does not present you based upon your offering...He presents you based upon your nature.

"But, Preacher, what about my actions?"

Your actions have no bearing on your nature.

In the Amplified Bible it reads:

> *Now to Him Who is able to keep you without stumbling or slipping or falling, and to present [you] unblemished (blameless and faultless) before the presence of His glory in triumphant joy and exultation [with unspeakable, ecstatic delight].*

Your spirit is incapable of holding a blemish because you are born of God (1 John 3:2). However, your flesh is not born of God. For example, if you were working on a car your hand would look greasy, but that grease has nothing to do with the nature of your hands.

When your spirit becomes born of God, you live from the inside, not the outside. So, if you get into some sin, it did not come by your spirit. You downshifted from your spirit to the flesh floor. That is why God says, "those who worship Me must worship Me in spirit." If you are worshipping in spirit, you are worshipping "in truth."

John 14:17 says, *"I am the way, the truth, and the life."* So, if I am worshipping Him in spirit and in truth, I am worshipping Him in Jesus where there is no darkness, only light.

Chapter Six: Your Lively Hope: Your Inheritance

THE CONDEMNATION COMPLEX

He that committeth sin is of the devil.
(1 John 3:8)

This is the Scripture the devil tries to use to put you in a condemnation complex. Many believe that "I've committed sin. Therefore, I must be of the devil."

This Scripture says "He that," and it is not talking about your flesh. If you never receive any revelation your whole life with God, remember that "he" and "you" are not flesh. You are not a soul. You are basically only a spirit.

He that committeth sin is of the devil; for the devil sinneth from the beginning.

For years I did not understand this Scripture. Now I know he is saying that the devil's nature is sin. That was the devil's nature in the beginning, and he will keep that nature.

It is not your nature to sin.

For this purpose the Son of God was manifested, that he might destroy the works of the devil.
(1 John 3:8)

"Destroy" means "to undo." You were in the flesh at one time (according to Ephesians 2:1). You were one of the children of disobedience. But when the purposes of the Son of God became manifest, He reached through His blood into your nature. He destroyed and abolished the old sin nature and put it on Himself.

He hung your old nature on the tree; He took it down to hell; He killed and destroyed it. He undid it inside of you so that you no longer had a fleshly, worldly, devilish nature.

Now if your nature is sin, you are not saved. The only nature you still have is the nature of God.

Whosoever is born of God doth not commit sin.
(Verse 9)

The Amplified Bible reads:

No one born (begotten) of God [deliberately, knowingly, and habitually] practices sin, for his seed remaineth [abides] in him.

When you live by God's nature, you don't ever want to sin. He that is born of God does not commit sin. Why? Because His nature abides in him.

God does not present you by your actions. Last week you may have become upset at someone who cut in front of you on the road.

God keeps you from falling.

The nature of Him inside of me reaches up and keeps me and says, "Don't say that."

When you want to go to the bar or strip club, something on the inside reaches up and gives you an out. He presents you, not by your actions, not by your behavior, but by your nature.

"But yesterday I caught that man in a lie."

"No you didn't, because he brought it to Me under the blood, and My Word says I forget it. I throw it behind My back as far as the east is from the west."

Chapter Six: Your Lively Hope: Your Inheritance

BEHAVIOR AND NATURE

There is a difference between behavior and nature. Nature is the sum total of an individual's character. Your nature is faultless, without blemish or stain, and it is your nature to experience victory.

Victory in your life should be as common as breathing.

In Hebrews 12 it says that they could not come near Mount Sinai because God's glory, God's power, God's anointing was all over that mountain. If even a goat strayed off course and touched that mountain, the power of God would kill him right there on the spot.

God is taking you into the Presence of His glory, right to the foot of the place. If any sin was in you, like that goat, it would die.

If you live by your nature, you can get to the foot of the cross. If you live by His nature, you can come right into the glory.

THE THREE SECTIONS

In the Old Covenant, there were three sections of the tabernacle:

1) the outer court,

2) the inner court, and

3) the Holy of Holies (the Most Holy Place). It was in the Most Holy Place that the Presence of God would manifest to the High Priest.

Hollywood tried to demonstrate the power of the Holy of Holies in the movie, "Raiders of the Lost Ark." In that movie, the glory of God burned a man to shreds. There is some level of truth to that.

History records that the High Priest would take a rope with him into the Holy of Holies with a bell on it every quarter of an inch. They would wrap the rope around his ankle so that when he walked into the Most Holy Place, if for some reason he were unclean and not able to stand in the Presence of God, they would hear a thud and the bells would go off. This would alert the people to pull him out. Then they would try and find another person who was spiritually qualified.

If God could not keep you, He would not present you as faultless in the Most Holy Place.

You might ask, "Well, Bishop, what does that mean?"

It means that God sent you into the Holy of Holies without bells on your ankles. He sent you in there knowing that you are going to come back. He knows you are clean and righteous in Him.

"But, Bishop, what about that sin I committed last week?"

That has no bearing on His blood!

You are covered, delivered, redeemed, rescued, kept and saved by His blood! The blood has never lost its power! It is the same blood yesterday, today and forever.

His blood has cleansed you.

God doesn't see you through the eyes of what you did yesterday.

If you live by your nature, your flesh cannot talk.

Chapter Six: Your Lively Hope: Your Inheritance

You have been crucified through Christ, and now your flesh is dead.

THE PAST IS PAST

"I can't help myself."

Oh, you better stop that. Your nature says you are under the blood. He presents you spotless in glory, with exceeding joy. It is not about the police report that says what you used to be. Your record has been expunged and your past erased. What you used to be yesterday does not exist.

What you used to say, you don't say any more.

Where you used to go, you don't go anymore.

You have been raised up by the blood of Jesus, born again by an incorruptible seed. The nature of God causes Him to present you faultless before the Presence of His glory with exceeding joy.

Erase the false impressions and failed evaluations. See yourself through the eyes of the blood.

You are kept through a lively hope.

You are kept from falling.

Whenever guilt tries to hold you down, whenever hard days try to take over your spirit, when depression comes knocking at your door, He is still keeping you from falling!

Whenever money is tight and your bank account does not look like fullness, when the rent is due and there's no money to pay it, when you feel like you are going down for the count, know that God is still keeping you!

The devil will tell you, "Listen, you should be able to go out and do what you used to do. You are justified because they're not treating you right. They are not saying the right things."

But God will keep you from falling.

Now, here's an important fact: you do not need to feel saved to act saved. You may never feel saved or clean.

That doesn't matter. It's not about your feelings!

Faith is not a feeling or an emotion. Faith is a fact.

The fact is that you are born again, not of corruptible seed, but of incorruptible seed by the Word of God which lives and abides in you forever.

Have you ever seen trophies that have the little inscriptions on the bottom? You know what Scripture says on your trophy?

"Unblemished."

Jesus says, "Father, I have a team, an offering."

"What is the name of the team?"

"Unblemished and faultless. I want to bring them into the glory."

God says, "Hallelujah, bring them on up in here. I don't see them through the eyes of their sin. Their sin is gone. I've thrown that behind My back as far as the east is from the west. I'm not waiting on them to fall someday, I'm keeping them."

Chapter Six: Your Lively Hope: Your Inheritance

The final line of the verse reads, "To the only wise God. His glory and majesty, dominion and power, now and forever, amen."

UNBLEMISHED, UNSPOTTED

He is not ashamed of you, and He no longer sees your sin. You are presented as faultless, so stop feeling guilty if you sin. Confess it, repent, and move on.

1 John 1:9 says,

If we confess our sins, he is faithful and just to forgive us our sins, and to cleanse us from all unrighteousness.

What is the unrighteousness? It is the feeling that comes after the fall. Someone reading this is now asking, "Why should I fall if He is able to keep me from falling?"

You shouldn't. You don't have to. It is your choice.

Stop falling and floundering in sin, swimming in a cesspool. Deal with your sin quickly, then move on. You cannot sin enough times to have a sinful nature.

Your nature is God's nature!

"Well, then, Bishop, how is it then that people lose their salvation?"

The difference between keeping salvation and losing it is caring. There wasn't a day when they suddenly said, "Oops, I'm not saved anymore." Those people did not care about a new nature. They completely walked away from that nature.

"But Bishop, I've reached the point of no return!"

How do you know that? Was there a mark in the road that said, "The point of no return"? It doesn't work like that. Now unto Him who is able to keep you from falling and present you without stain, without blemish, before the Presence of His glory with exceeding joy, laughing at the devil the whole way.

Chapter Seven

The Blessings of Renewal

God is keeping us by His power and His miraculous force. As He does, change begins to take place in us. We change our confessions, our confidence level, and our understanding level. We begin to thank the Lord for keeping us from accidents, negative incidents, and unfortunate coincidences.

You start to live in a certain direction, with a certain outcome that God has already given you because you have an inheritance that is incorruptible, undefiled, and does not fade away!

As God begins to do a work in you, He starts to put within you the need to service certain areas of your life that have gone untouched.

Years ago, one of the first things I noticed was that there were areas in me that God needed to touch and minister to. One of them that I shared in another chapter was my situation with Erik. Of course, there were many other areas that impacted my emotional well-being, my physical well-being, my mental well-being, and my financial well-being.

So many areas needed addressing.

You may be the child of a single-parent household, but you don't have to wear the scars of that situation.

You may have had a father who abandoned you, but you no longer need to feel alone.

You may have had serious health problems throughout your life, but God is here to heal you.

Your problems mean nothing when they are placed in the hands of the Almighty Creator of the universe!

You may have had a situation that scarred you, causing you to be in a dysfunctional state, but Jesus can handle it!

God is willing to change every area of your life that needs changing, but here's the catch: He won't change it until you get to the place where you recognize the problem inside.

He'll start changing you when you start noticing He has kept you by the power.

My Spirit of Intimidation

The first thing God does is put within us the need to service certain areas in our lives that have gone untouched.

The second thing He does is reach into us and bring the need to the forefront. The reason He does this is because you can't begin to pray over a thing when you don't know what the problem is.

The instant I began to deal with specific areas in my life, the Holy Spirit started to show me certain specific pictures that held meaning for me. One of the first that came before me was a picture from the fifth grade.

I saw a little boy come up to me. I clearly remembered his looming presence over me. He was a bully. I remember feeling intimidation and humiliation. There was something inside of me that began to "power down" in this bully's presence.

Years later, someone in the church came before me with that same type of intimidating spirit and something within me waffled. Although today I thank God for that experience, I immediately recognized that this picture was from the fifth grade.

Why was that picture brought to my remembrance?

Because God was ready to do something in me. I began to sense anger come over me, but I didn't have the courage to deal with it.

INTIMIDATION'S CONTROL

Some of you reading this book may be on jobs where you are being incredibly taken advantage of, but you are too afraid to step out into something better. I don't mean you need to walk away from your job, I mean you need to start preparing yourself to land something better. You need to start getting your resume updated.

If you need a career that is going to pay you better, if

you need someone who is going to treat you better, then now is your time to start getting yourself together.

If you know you're not making the best amount of money, not employed in the best company, do not have the best position, then start getting yourself some training so you can go elsewhere. Get yourself so prepared that the place you are at right now will need to kick you out because you are suddenly too qualified to be there. Get yourself to a place that's going to be glad to have you.

I remember seeing these things take place in me. In my prayer time, God began to bring things to the forefront of my mind.

Why?

Because whatever comes to the surface, that is the stuff you can start working on. Not only does God bring it to the forefront, He incorporates it into your prayer time. You'll be praying for something else and He'll start bringing that stuff back to your mind.

God reminded me of that same spirit of intimidation I went through in the fifth grade. I thought, "Why is this thing bothering me? I'm not even thinking about that little picky-haired boy!" But picky-haired boys grow up to be picky-haired men.

The spirit of intimidation that makes a boy cower down is the same spirit of intimidation that makes an adult cower down. And, the same spirit of intimidation that makes Christians cower down comes from the devil.

If you cower down then, then you are going to cower down when God is trying to lead you somewhere else if you do not know you're kept. He brings it up during your prayer time so that you can find the perfect will of God on that subject for your life.

Praying in the Spirit

God perfects that which concerns you.

When you know you are kept in everything that concerns you, God perfects it. God covers your smile. Even if you don't have one, God covers it. He is willing to do whatever it takes to get your best smile back because He always perfects that which concerns you as you are kept by God.

> *Likewise the Spirit also helpeth our infirmities: for we know not what we should pray for as we ought: but the Spirit itself maketh intercession for us with groanings which cannot be uttered." Cannot be uttered in known speech. And he that searcheth the hearts knoweth what is the mind of the Spirit, because he maketh intercession for the saints according to the will of God.*
> (Romans 8:26,27)

Some say, "But I don't understand what is going on when I am praying in tongues. I don't understand this thing. Is it gibberish?"

When you are praying in the Spirit, it's not you who is praying, it is the Spirit of God praying within you. You have been given the voice, you have been given the will, and you have engaged the mechanism.

When you agree to speak His language out of your mouth, what you are praying for is precisely whatever the perfect will of God is for your life.

God starts activating His will in you.

While you are praying in tongues, praying in agreement with the Holy Ghost, God is orchestrating and configuring whatever it is going to take to bring His perfect will into your life.

You say, "But while I was praying, I started thinking about that new job."

Remember, you're kept by the power. When you begin praying in the Holy Ghost, then God starts shifting you to get you to that new job.

I like to call it "putting divine discontentment" in you—where the highest check you make on that job will never be the best check you know you can make.

Then you will begin noticing that if God wants you to stay there, positions will begin to open up to you, opportunities will start opening up.

The Activated Power of the Holy Ghost

You pray in the Holy Ghost.

Why?

Because when you pray in the Holy Ghost, you activate the power — the same power that keeps you. If the power can keep you, the power can lead you. And if the power can lead you, the power can direct you. And if the power can direct you, you can receive the perfect will of God.

God says that He who searches the heart knows what is in the Spirit's mind. Therefore, when I begin praying

Chapter Seven: The Blessings of Renewal

in the Spirit, He begins to make intercession according to the will of God.

You may say, "I want to know what God's perfect will is about a particular subject. What do I need to do?"

Well, you don't need to go find a palm reader. It won't work.

"But, Bishop, I believe God is ready for me to have a mate."

He may be, but you aren't going to get one by searching for your spouse. If you search for your spouse through your flesh, you are going to pick up someone in the flesh.

A young lady called me one time and said, "You just don't want anybody happy but you."

"No," I replied as kindly as I could, "I'm just tired of saints having too many trash days."

Trash days for many are every single day of the week because that's how they choose to live — from one trashy situation to the next.

PRAY FOR GOD'S WILL

A young lady who left the church said, "I want to tell you something. I don't want you to call me out about my loose fiancée."

"Fiancée" is frequently a nice word for "somebody that I'm already messing around with." This lady then said to me, "Bishop, I don't want anyone telling me nothing about how I live. I don't want anybody telling him about anything either. Besides, I might not marry him."

"That's a sign right there," I replied, "that you are living trash days throughout the week."

Child of God, if you want to find a mate, then don't even look. Look for the perfect will of God, not for the perfect mate.

Begin to pray in the Holy Ghost, and God will begin to shape you up for the person you are going to have. You do not want to be in sin one day, and be praying that God will keep you the next day.

Some people just can't live without someone, and then when they get them, they are ready to dump them at the next bus stop. But when you are praying in the Holy Ghost, you are praying the absolute perfect will of God for all situations.

You may ask, "Why, Bishop?"

Because the same power of the Spirit is the same Spirit's power that keeps you.

HE RENEWS MY STRENGTH

The next thing that begins to happen is you receive revelation. He begins to keep it before you until you do something about it. In other words, when you're being kept by the power, He begins to take you through the process of renewal, restoration and redemption.

If I'm renewed, restored and redeemed, I begin to receive a revelation! I am kept by the power. He is then all over me and He's keeping me alive.

Chapter Seven: The Blessings of Renewal

When He keeps you by the power, He takes you through a process called renewal.

> *But they that wait upon the LORD shall renew their strength; they shall mount up with wings as eagles; they shall run, and not be weary; and they shall walk, and not faint.*
>
> (Isaiah 40:31)

He shall renew my strength because when I am being kept by the power, so a very interesting thing happens to me concerning my power and strength.

Let's dissect those words.

Take three strands of cord and begin to twirl them around each other. Soon they become one strand, and it becomes difficult to see them individually. You can't tell if it's three different strands because they have all become one.

> *And if one prevail against him, two shall withstand him; and a threefold cord is not quickly broken.*
>
> (Ecclesiastes 4:12)

As God brings you through His process of renewal, your spirit is woven with His like a three-fold cord, and in that spiritual miracle, you become far stronger as a new "one" than you ever were individually on your own.

The Hebrew word for "they that wait upon the Lord" is "kayil" which means to whirl. The word "kayil" is actually a term we use for dance; yet, it is also the same word we use for travail. And, ladies, travail is the same thing you did when the doctor said, "Push." When he said "Push," everything about you began to focus on what was in you; all you wanted to do was to get that baby out. You wanted to get it away, far away from you.

And so, those who are woven together with God shall renew their strength and soar like eagles!

They who are in a travailing (pregnant) situation with God will be renewed.

A Greater Destiny

"Bishop, when He's renewing me, am I kept by the power?"

Yes, God has impregnated you with His Spirit when you are kept by the power! He takes the secrets of His heart, He takes the desires of His mind, He takes the future, your destiny, and He somehow stuffs it up in your womb! If you pursue this revelation of being kept by the power, you will begin to understand that you are pregnant with God's heart for you.

The more you realize you are kept by the power, the more you are pregnant with His heart. You begin to understand that you are not just trying to be something because some preacher told you that you could have something in God. You begin to understand that the more you develop a relationship with Him, the more He starts putting greatness and His divine destiny in front of you.

It's not because you begged Him for these spiritual transformations, but because you are one with His Spirit, He begins to renew your strength. The word "renew" means "to exchange"...you begin to exchange your earthly nature for His Godly nature.

They that *kahil* – whirl, dance, push – become impregnated by God, shall "slide by" their strength.

"Bishop, what do you mean, 'slide by'"?

"Slide by" is another Hebrew translation. A fuller definition is "slide by, cut off, grow up beyond."

Think about it. Isn't that what all believers are trying to do? To cut off, to slide past, to grow beyond ourselves and to draw closer to Him?

As He cuts you off from your old man, God wants you to soar like an eagle, to be so closely entwined with Him that you are literally like a woven cord that is not easily broken.

KEPT BY HIS MIRACULOUS POWER

Have you ever said to yourself, "If I could just grow up beyond my own strength. If God could just get me to the end of myself, I could be somebody in the Lord because the truth is the life"?

You can and will grow beyond yourself as you begin to understand that you're kept by the power, by His miraculous force.

The word "power" means "the miraculous force of God." You are going to find that this power is the same power that parted the Red Sea, that flooded the earth for forty days and nights, that brought Lazarus from the dead, that brought Jesus out of His grave.

Romans 8:11 declares that:

The same Spirit that raised Christ from the dead dwells in you, He that raised Christ from the dead will quicken your mortal body by His Spirit that dwells in you.

Now that's exciting! He will bring life to your mortal body by His Spirit that dwells in you. He wanted to give you life so desperately that Jesus went to hell on your behalf. When Jesus was on the cross, He took everything you deserved upon Himself.

You deserved hell.

So, for three days, that's where Jesus went. He went to hell to serve your prison term of eternity away from God. The devil was full of glee because He thought that Jesus was the Son of God, but he wasn't really sure. The first day and night when Jesus was in hell, Satan must have said to himself, "Well, nothing's happening with Him. He couldn't be the Son of God. He's just like any other person. But I *think* He's the Son of God. Well, like I said, nothing's happening.

"All of these prophecies that the priests, the prophets and the books have said about Him exploding this place, messing everything up. . .well, I don't think so. There's a dead man here, and He's got sin on Him."

The second day and night and still nothing happens.

"Just like I thought. He's still not doing nothing."

Understand, most believe that Jesus raised Himself from the dead.

He didn't.

He couldn't.

Chapter Seven: The Blessings of Renewal

PRESENTED IN GLORY

Jesus was immobilized because He had our sins on Him. Jesus was raised from the dead by the glory of the Father, and that same glory is the same power that caused darkness to be light, the same glory spoken of in Jude 1:24:

Now unto him that is able to keep you from falling, and to present you faultless before the presence of his glory.

It is that same glory God wants to place in your presence. It is that same glory God used to raise Jesus from the dead. It is that same glory that Jesus uses to present you as faultless before the Father as He keeps you!

When Jesus presents you to the glory, He's not presenting you as a stranger. He took the glory in you and presented it to the glory of His Presence, raising you up by the glory of the Father.

Imagine...Jesus literally reached down into hell so He could raise you up!

RENEWED BY HIS GLORY

Now, that same Spirit also quickens your mortal body. "Quicken" means "to bring life to," "to renew." You are renewed by the Spirit of God. You are renewed by the glory of the Father.

They that wait upon the Lord shall exchange their strength, shall grow beyond their strength, shall be over their strength, shall pass by their strength.

One Hebrew definition states that "they shall strike through their strength." Have you ever made a mistake on a piece of paper. You wrote it in ink, and of course, you had no white-out anywhere around? All you could do was strike through it and write the correction on top of that strike out.

God is saying here, "As long as you're in yourself, then you're operating on your own strength. But when you understand that you're *kept by MY power*, you strike through your own strength and put MY strength on top of that. You are renewed!"

His Glorious Restoration

When you are kept by His power, you are restored.

Friend, there's a difference between the words "renew" and "restore." Every time the word "restore" is found in the Bible, it has a different meaning than "renew."

"Restore" is mentioned for the first time in Psalm 23:3-4:

> *He restoreth my soul: he leadeth me in the paths of righteousness for his name's sake. Yea, though I walk through the valley of the shadow of death.*

Notice the word "through." Some of us might want to camp out or set up residence in the valley, but God never intended for that to happen. He wanted you to walk *through* the valley of the shadow of death!

Pray for peace in the valley, but hear God when He tells you to walk through it. Psalm 23:4 continues: *"Yea, though I walk through the valley of the shadow of death,*

Chapter Seven: The Blessings of Renewal

I will fear no evil." You do not fear evil in the valley, it can't get you, because you are *kept by the power*!

Nowhere in the Bible does it provide a place for you to be riddled by fear. There is no provision for you to be struggling in shortage, or left lifeless by lies. There is no provision for the enemy to have his scrawny thumb pressing down on you.

The Bible declares that the devil is under your feet! It is time we walk in the revelation that even ONE of your feet is large enough to squash the devil!

The Bible declares that the devil is a pathetic worm who is destined to be pulverized by your feet, whether they are big or small. Whether your feet are as big as Shaquille O'Neal's or as small as an infant's, they are crushing all of Satan all of the time.

I will fear no evil: for thou art with me. Thy rod and thy staff they comfort me.

God promises He is not going to leave you by yourself, and without comfort. Instead, He wants to renew and restore you!

Continued Service

The first word for "restore" in the Hebrew means "to turn back without having to start over."

"Bishop, do you mean that when I begin to get a revelation that He's keeping me by the power, He's turning me back?"

Yes, He is.

He's turning you back to look at the things you don't have that you're supposed to have. He's turning you back and giving you a chance to start over without starting over. He's turning you back and giving you continued service on the things you're supposed to be enjoying right now.

When Jesus restores, He means for you to turn back without having to start over, to fetch home again, to find out what's supposed to be yours and to command it to come on back home.

Tell that blessing to get on back here!

Increase, get on back here!

Deliverance, come on back here! You belong to me!

Why is it that we wake up, look up, and find ourselves five, six or seven years down the road without the things we believed we were supposed to be having?

Say this next sentence out loud and let it sink deep into your spirit.

"God never intended me to be where I am when where I am is beneath where He wants me to be."

Now, say it again with more conviction and power.

"God never intended me to be where I am when where I am is beneath where He wants me to be."

Is the Holy Spirit starting to speak to you right now? Are you beginning to realize that when you are kept by His Spirit, you are destined to be something more than you are today?

Chapter Seven: The Blessings of Renewal

As God renews, restores and redeems you, you will never be the same again.

Friends will ask, "What happened to you?" and you will say, "I've been renewed, restored and redeemed by Jesus Christ who died for me, went to hell for me, and now is bringing me to the place I never thought I could go."

Get ready.

Your past is done.

Your present is not your future.

Your future is where God wants you to be.

Chapter Eight

Restoration: Servicing Areas We Don't See

"Restore" means "to beckon home again."

You can't tell your dog to "get back home" if you don't know he is gone!

You can't get your health back if you are so used to being sick that you have forgotten how to get back to health.

You can't command a higher standard in your life if being beaten down is the only standard you know in your life.

About a year ago I was praying over an issue that I was believing God for, but became too busy to properly monitor the situation. When you believe God for something, you had better be a good steward and monitor the things God has entrusted you with.

I told myself, "Well, I'm just going to have to get ready to start believing for that situation another time." The second I said that, the Spirit of God spoke to me and asked, "Why?"

"What did you say?"

"Why?" the Spirit of God replied. "You're kept by the power. And because you're *kept by the power*, the things that belong to you are yours. You're *kept by the power*, so before you even think about what's gone, I'll be bringing it back."

The second God said that, I replied, "Hold on to that thought, Lord. Let me run to my office. I've got to find out what you just said."

Sometimes we become so accustomed to thinking "it's not going to come to pass" because we haven't seen it coming. But, God would have us to service the things we don't see.

For example, what if you arrive at the drive-through bank, and you start to let the window down in your car, but it doesn't go down. It fails to work. So, you compromise and say, "I guess I'll just be walking in from now on" instead of getting the window fixed.

When we don't service the areas of our lives we don't readily see, that gives the enemy grounds to lull us into complacency, getting us used to living without restoration, without renewal, without the full redemption power God desires for us.

THE SEVEN-YEAR FAMINE

"Restoration" also means "to refresh, to relieve again, to rest again."

God's ready to bring you into a state of rest.

Chapter Eight: Restoration

The second word for restoration (there are four of them) comes from 2 Kings 8:1,

> *Then spake Elisha unto the woman, whose son he had restored to life, saying, Arise, and go thou and thine household, and sojourn wheresoever thou canst sojourn: for the LORD hath called for a famine; and it shall also come upon the land seven years. And the woman arose, and did after the saying of the man of God: and she went with her household, and sojourned in the land of the Philistines seven years. And it came to pass at the seven years' end, that the woman returned out of the land of the Philistines: and she went forth to cry unto the king for her house and for her land.*

The woman went back to the King because she had to leave the land due to the seven-year famine.

Now, after seven years of famine, she wants to go back and retrieve her land.

> *And the king talked with Gehazi the servant of the man of God, saying, Tell me, I pray thee, all the great things that Elisha hath done. And it came to pass, as he was telling the king how he had restored a dead body to life, that, behold, the woman, whose son he had restored to life, cried to the king for her house and for her land. And Gehazi said, 'My lord, O king, this is the woman, and this is her son, whom Elisha restored to life.' And when the king asked the woman, she told him. So the king appointed unto her a certain officer, saying, Restore all that was hers, and all the fruits of the field since the day that she left the land, even until now.*

Do you see it?

Even though the woman had been gone seven years, she left trying to make sure that the famine didn't come upon her and her seed. She came back after the famine was gone, asking for everything she had during that seven-year period of time. Not only did she ask for everything she had, but she wanted it to be *restored to the same condition* she left it in!

When you recognize that you're *kept by the power*, God begins to restore inside of you things that have deteriorated over the years. He begins to bring you back to the higher standard.

It doesn't matter what you got into ruin over. It doesn't matter what you descended into. It doesn't matter if you have plummeted downward the last two or three years of your life. God doesn't see that decline.

The moment you know you're kept by the power is when that glorious power inside of you begins to push you back up above your declined state. The king assigned an officer to this woman and said, *"Restore unto this woman all that is hers, and even give her the fruits of her ground."* In other words, if there was any harvest for that woman when she left the place seven years ago, give it all back to her too.

God is saying, "Whatever belongs to you is all yours."

Maybe you had to run like a thief in the night. Maybe your time was stolen. Maybe your job was taken. Maybe you had to walk away from that money. But God is saying, "No, it's all yours. I'm restoring all of this to you."

Chapter Eight: Restoration

Is Somebody Stealing From You?

The third word for "restore" appears in Proverbs 6:31. It is a very familiar Scripture. We know this Word because it tells us about thieves.

> *Men do not despise a thief if he steal to satisfy his soul when he is hungry; But if he be found, he shall restore sevenfold; he shall give all the substance of his house.*
>
> (Proverbs 6:30-31)

The Hebrew word "restore" here means "to be made safe in mind, body, or estate."

"Bishop, what in the world are you saying?"

I'm saying it means to make restitution until prosperity comes! If you know the devil's taking from you, don't sit there and say, "I wonder how long the devil is going to take from me." If you don't have what God says is yours, then somebody is stealing from you. If he be caught, if he be found, then the Word says he shall restore to you sevenfold, seven times the worth, the value, of what you lost.

"But, Bishop, I lost a car."

Seven times the loss.

"But the car I had wasn't that good."

Well, what it was worth, increase it by seven times.

Stop thinking that you can't buy a new car off the lot. Wisdom tells you there is nothing wrong with getting a used car. But, if all you've had all your life is a used car, and thought you could never do any better, then it might be in your best interest to drive a car that has never been driven before.

Want It Back, Seven Times the Value

"Bishop, why should I want it back seven times?"

Just to know that God will do it for you.

"Well, then, what exactly is 'the sevenfold restora-restoration?'"

Seven times better the mindset. Seven times higher the attitude. Seven times better the knowledge and understanding. Seven times the attitude, "If anybody is going to get it, I ought to have it because I'm a child of God."

If anybody ought to drive it, I ought to drive it.
If anybody is going to live in it, I ought to live in it.
If anybody is going to enjoy it, I ought to enjoy it.

When a person in our church buys a new home, my wife always advises, "Don't take that old trash into that new home." She's right. If that stuff is keeping you down, it is trash.

Of course, your trash may be somebody else's treasure. But if it's one of those sofas that is so worn out that you lose people in it, it couldn't be anybody's treasure. Get rid of it.

God will restore sevenfold.

Remember, verse 31 says, *"He shall restore sevenfold; he shall give all the substance of his house."*

"What do you mean, Bishop?"

Chapter Eight: Restoration

I mean that when you get a revelation that you're *kept by the power*, you will bankrupt the effects of the devil. You are going to shut down his operation that steals from you because God is going to give you restitution until you are prosperous!

The devil's got to keep paying you back until there's nothing left in his coffers. Everything in the devil's cabinets belong to you. You can start declaring, "Devil, you just keep making restitution to me until there is nothing that has my name on it in your coffers, shelves or inventory. It's all mine and it belongs to me."

It may be an old mud doll you played with when you were three years old and some child stole it. "I want my mud doll back with seven times the greater value. It all belongs to me."

GETTING MY REVELATION

The fourth word for "restoration" is found in the very powerful verses of Jeremiah 30:16-17,

Therefore all they that devour thee shall be devoured; and all thine adversaries, every one of them, shall go into captivity; and they that spoil thee shall be a spoil, and all that prey upon thee will I give for a prey. For I will restore health unto thee, and I will heal thee of thy wounds, saith the LORD; because they called thee an outcast, saying, This is Zion, whom no man seeketh after. Thus saith the LORD; Behold, I will bring again the captivity of Jacob's tents.

In other words, God is saying, "Whatever was in your tents I'm going to bring back to you. It's all yours. I'm going to restore your health and I'm going to remove your wounds."

Here, the word "restore" means to ascend. It is as if God is saying, "I'm going to cause everything about you to be ascended into a higher realm, a higher level, a higher tax bracket."

Now don't go getting upset about higher taxes. That just means God is going to bless you and you're going to make more. How can you get upset about that?

Even the new, higher taxes you pay will be a blessing to others as you do your part to take care of the roads you drive on, the bridges you cross, and the pot holes that need repairing all over your city.

This word also means "to cause to ascend."

In other words, God is causing you to ascend to your restoration. God is saying, "I'll restore your health and remove your wounds. I'm going to cause you to ascend above hell, above sickness."

This blessing rubs off. When others get near you, you are going to cause them to ascend too because you are *kept by the power*, and that power is infectious! When you start to walk in this revelation, you will start rising above sickness and lack, rising above poverty, rising above shortage, rising above bondage, and rising above imprisonment.

GOD IS BRINGING ASCENSION TO YOU

As you change, others around you will start to rise above the things in their own lives without knowing

Chapter Eight: Restoration

what is happening to them. They'll just know they started to change and become better because you are their friend.

When you started being their friend, their money started breaking loose. Their happiness started coming. Their family started acting right. Their peace started coming. They started having nights of real rest.

Why?

Because you are kept by the power and that power is large enough to impact your friends!

Get ready.

When you ascend, you ascend at once. Your day is literally disrupted because of your personal ascension.

"What do you mean, Bishop?"

I mean God's going to interrupt your schedule and bring ascension to you. I mean that right in the middle of wherever you are on your way to, God is about to give you a collision of ascension because you are kept by the power.

"But, Bishop, do I have to believe a certain thing, or quote a certain thing, or confess a certain thing?"

No.

You just have to know a certain thing. You have to know that you're *kept by the power*. One day you'll be looking up at what you want to have, and the next day you'll be looking down at what you ought to have. Then you'll realize that on the day you were looking up, you were far from it. You couldn't see yourself with it. But on the next day, you started looking down and exclaimed, "Oh, that belongs to me!" You will find yourself looking down so you can select what's yours.

"It's mine."

Restored.

You do not need to drive through the nice neighborhoods anymore and go hoping and praying that the day is going to come when that home can belong to you. Instead, you will begin to find yourself looking down at the neighborhood and stepping into what you want. You will be designing what you want, begin to assign what you want, and be ready to enjoy what you want because nobody can keep you from what is already yours.

INCREASE SHALL BE YOURS

While you're ascending, you're growing up over into increase.

"You mean to tell me that all I have to do is understand the revelation of being *kept by the power?*"

Let me give you a simple example to demonstrate my point. At school, there were girls who thought they had to act snooty and snobby to be a part of the exclusive club of do-nothings. Now, over the weekend one of them (we will call her Molly) gets a revelation that she is *kept by the power*.

Molly goes back to school on a Monday and guess what? She no longer strives to come down to her friends' level. On the contrary. Molly now realizes that her friends need to "come up" to her standard if they want to run with her. They start asking, "What club do you

Chapter Eight: Restoration

belong to now? What keeps you doing what you're doing and looking like you're looking?"

Molly wisely replies, "Well, it is the 'kept club.' I'm *kept by the power*. Things have changed here. Oh, I'll let you get in, but you have to come through my Daddy first."

"Restored" also means "to spring up." Notice the immediacy in that term? You suddenly spring up. Have you ever jumped and caused somebody to be startled or to spring up?

The dead heads (excuse the expression) around you are used to you being with them. They look around, and all of a sudden they are darkness and you are light. All of a sudden you have received the revelation that you are kept by the power and increase shall be yours.

You're Going to "Pop"!

Suddenly, somebody springs up.

Pop!

The Hebrew word is "sock you." As I began to look through the Hebrew translations, the only way I can adequately translate this Hebrew word is to define what happens to a kernel of corn inside of a microwave when it hits the right temperature. It doesn't matter if it looks like a big old seed one minute. All of a sudden, "pop"! You're going to have popcorn. That's what God wants us to do, to get a revelation that we're kept by the power and then pop.

I don't care if you look like a closed-up seed. I don't care if all you look like is a drab, unfulfilled, bankrupted, foreclosed, repossessed seed. When you receive the right temperature, when you get the right revelation, you're going to pop!

You're going to shock.

You're going to get some folks scared.

Then they are going to follow you wherever you go. Things are going to be different. You will not look the same way after you pop.

Your bills will get paid now. Pop. You're going to pull up in the driveway with something new. Pop. You're going to put a "For Sale" sign in the yard. Pop.

Everything is going to be bright again. Your marriage is going to be on top again. All the promotions are coming to you. Pop. Pop. Pop.

When nobody else is getting a raise, you're going to get one. You're going to ascend at once. It's going to be the breaking of day.

There'll be Some Changes Made

Soon, I expect to receive letters from people reading this book, sharing how this revelation has changed their lives. One will read:

"Bishop Coleman,

"Oh what joy is breaking forth, coming forth, shouting forth in my soul. I'm being restored. I'm being recovered. I'm being repaired. My friends don't know what's happened to me. They still don't know why I've changed. All they understand is I looked closed one day,

Chapter Eight: Restoration

then one day the heat got on me, the right temperature got on me, and I started popping. I started popping. I started changing.

"Things are different now. I used to be real quiet with not much to say. But then all of a sudden, something started happening inside of me. Something started moving through me.

"What was on the inside started moving to the outside. God on the inside started changing me on the outside.

"I started popping. I popped right out of Payless. I popped right out of the blue light specials. I popped right out of the bargain basement because I realized I was kept by the power.

"I was kept by the force of God. I was kept by the resurrection life. I was kept by the glory which means to shoot up, to burn.

"Bishop Coleman, thank you for this revelation."

Friend, you can't keep quiet when the right temperature rises. You can't keep quiet. They call it a critical burn, a critical mass, when a cell reaches the right temperature and it begins to split and multiply.

When you begin to experience the right temperature, the right heat, everything God puts in you will start multiplying.

Chapter Nine

Redemption: Redeeming What You've Lost

When God begins to bring renewal into your life, He ushers in restoration, and finally, He begins to bring you redemption.

I'm redeemed. That word is found in Ephesians 5:16. It says, *"Redeeming the time, because the days are evil."* The Amplified Bible reads, *"Making the very most of the time [buying up each opportunity], because the days are evil."*

The Greek word here means "to rescue from being lost." The inference is that whenever you receive a revelation that you're *kept by the power*, God begins to assign an angel to you who begins to go through the corridors, boundaries and perimeters of my past.

You begin to find all the opportunities you lost, all the things that were supposed to be yours. That angel begins to find places where you had a business deal but lost it, where you had a money-making opportunity, but lost it, where you had earned a scholarship, but lost it.

He begins to find where you had a good thing going, but lost it, where you had money that was owed to you, but lost it, where you had a friend, and lost him. He found where you had a situation that was supposed to be yours, where you were supposed to come out on top, but you came out at the bottom.

That angel is going to be walking with you the second you know you are *kept by the power*. He's going to buy up those opportunities because you're kept. You just stand there and the angel reaches into his pocket and buys you back that opportunity.

My Mama's Death

When I was nine years old, we had to leave my house because my mother was riddled with cancer. We didn't understand what cancer was, and could not comprehend how it had taken over her body. We didn't understand the years of neglect to her physical frame.

We moved in with my oldest sister, and late one night at 11:45 p.m. the phone rang. My sister immediately began to cry.

My oldest brother gathered us all together on the king-sized bed. I remember him looking over to us and saying, "Momma is gone." We all looked at each other and denied it.

Just then my oldest sister walked by the door and we could hear her crying. She said, "You all go ahead and get up now, we got to go somewhere."

We slowly dressed, each one of us trying to comprehend what had just happened. I was the youngest, and said, "I think Mama is gone."

Chapter Nine: Redemption

"Uh-uh, my brother said, "It couldn't be. Mama ain't gone."

Then I remember driving away in that old Chevy Caprice. While riding down the road I could see my sister with her head in her hands, but she was not telling us anything. We began instinctively to feel the total emptiness.

It's happened. When we got to the house, there were other cars already in the driveway. Where Mama had slept in her hospital bed inside the house, there were two relatives standing at the door to keep us from being able to look in the room.

I remember, as the youngest child, there was access around the side of the house. When I tried to run around, somebody was standing there. I remember stooping down and crawling through the ledge, and running to the side of that bed.

Then I remember how my whole world fell right out of my body. I felt the emptiness, the void, the deep hole, because as I looked down at her still frame, every memory there seemed to be lost.

Everything was gone at that moment.

My World Fell Apart

I remember running as they tried to catch me. I began to scream out, and I learned for the first time that it was possible for someone to cry past the fluid in their system; I had cried until blood was coming out of my eyes.

I remember trying to deal with this at the age of nine.

The worst thing was, the day of the funeral was my birthday.

Death comes at unexpected times. From that day forward I associated birthdays with loss, and loss with pain, and pain with shortage and shortage with the removal of the things you love the most.

After that, I remember having some very bizarre relationships because I couldn't love deeply and I didn't know why. I remember being very affectionate on one hand, and abusive on the other. And I didn't know why.

I could love somebody one minute and hate their guts the next, and I didn't know why. When I received Jesus at almost eighteen years of age, I remember calling a lady "Mama" and she called me "Baby."

One day she said, "Baby, let me tell you something. God has to give you a Momma again so you can handle it right now."

"What are you talking about?" I asked.

"You don't know how to love," she replied, "because when you did love, it was taken from you. What you loved was removed from you. So God has got to help you."

She began to pray in the Holy Ghost. I never knew what praying in tongues was all about, but as she prayed, I began to notice something happening on the inside of me.

God Bought Back Time in My Life

I noticed my spirit man began to feel like Somebody

was welding me with a torch. This Somebody was beginning to burn out the pain, cauterizing all of the suffering, removing all of the wounds, and taking away all of the things I had lost.

Over the years, God has given me other mothers. He Himself has been an incredible Father and Mother to me. I look at my mother-in-law, and she's more than a mother-in-law to me.

God began to reach all the way back, over almost thirty years of ministry, and started to buy back time in my life.

For you, maybe it is a former relationship that ended in divorce. Maybe there are some things you think you could have done differently.

But trust me, you can't go back to get that person. What you've got to do is let God buy back the time. Maybe you did some things as a sinner that now, as a parent, have cost you your children. Maybe you lost that thing, but when you've got a revelation that He is keeping you by the power, understand that now He is buying back the time.

Maybe you know your Momma, but your Daddy walked out on you. Maybe your Momma raised you. Maybe there were no real father figures in your life, so you became afraid of anything male, masculine, or manly. But God will take His angel and buy back the time. All you need is a revelation that He is keeping you by the power.

HE WILL RESCUE YOUR EVERY LOSS

When you get a revelation, He will take you through renewal, restoration and redemption. He will rescue every loss you ever had. He will let you slide by your strength.

You will pick up His strength. He will cause you to pop like popcorn and you will understand it's not about what you do, it's not about what you confess, it's all about what you know.

You are free from every evil work. You are all kept by the power, free from all decline.

> *To an inheritance incorruptible, and undefiled, and that fadeth not away, reserved in heaven for you, Who are kept by the power of God through faith unto salvation ready to be revealed in the last time.*
>
> (1 Peter 1:4-5)

In the Amplified it reads, "*[Born anew] into an inheritance which is beyond the reach of change.*" Do you see it? Your inheritance is beyond the reach of change.

What is an inheritance? It is something somebody has left for you that has been passed down.

The earthly inheritance we receive is sometimes subject to deterioration, but God tells us that we have an inheritance that is beyond the reach of change. He goes on to say, it "*is beyond the reach of change and decay [imperishable], unsullied and unfading, reserved in heaven for you.*"

Now, verse five in the Amplified says, "*Who are being guarded (garrisoned) by God's power.*"

Chapter Nine: Redemption

Notice, you are surrounded by God's power!

What do you think happens when you're surrounded by God's power?

Nothing gets through. Nothing gets in, and nothing gets out either. Not only can evil not enter you, but your standard is intact within you. So, when God declares that you are being garrisoned or surrounded by His power, then no one can take away from you the very high standard you maintain in God.

Kept at the Level of God's Promise and Desire

I stumbled upon a revelation of this verse one day when I made a comment to the Lord. I said, "Oops, I haven't remembered to believe You for so-and-so, so I guess I'll have to do this-and-that."

What I was saying is, "I guess I'll have to get something lesser because I waited too long."

God's response was quick.

"Don't you understand you're kept at the same level? You are not only kept to receive the things of God, but you are kept to receive at the same level."

What level?

You are kept at the TOP level of God's desire. In other words, whatever God desires for you, you've been kept at that level.

But you say, "What if I sin?"

You're kept at that level.

Sin is an action and righteousness is a nature. You have the nature of righteousness within you. You have to separate your behavior from your nature. You've been kept at the level of God's desire.

And, you've been kept at the level of God's promise. Whatever He promised you, whether it is a good day, a meaningful job, you're kept at the level of God's blessings. That is His promise to you. It doesn't matter how long it takes you to get it.

And, the delay will never be in God.

CHOOSE A LIFE OF PEACE

Many years ago Kenneth Hagin said, "After I had been pastoring for twelve years, the Lord spoke to me and said, 'Well, now you've entered into the first phase of your ministry.'"

"What?" Hagin replied, "I've been doing this for twelve years."

Whatever you've been doing," the Lord replied, "you obviously have not entered into the first phase yet. You've been going through the motions and have yet to step into the right place."

You can tell the difference between a person who enjoys each year of their life and one who considers their life drudgery.

They have peace in their life. They aren't picking up the phone every couple of minutes to see if there's still a dial tone. They aren't putting the car key in and clicking it a couple of times in the ignition to see if it's going to start.

Chapter Nine: Redemption

Now is your time to stop going year-to-year, from crisis-to-crisis, from hard time to hard time, and now is your time to decide that you are going to live a peaceful, productive life, beyond anything you've experienced before.

Jesus said in Matthew 11:30, *"My yoke is easy and my burden is light."* There's a place in Him, whenever we begin to stop going through the motions and start really living life.

"What do you mean?" you might ask.

The same verse that says "my yoke is easy" reads this way in the Amplified Bible:

For My yoke is wholesome (useful, good--not harsh, hard, sharp, or pressing, but comfortable, gracious, and pleasant), and My burden is light and easy to be borne.

It brings you recreation. When I think of recreation, I think of getting up because I want to, and staying up because I want to.

That is what God desires for all of us.

God wants you to live in the full experience of His peace and promise.

God wants you to love your days and relish your nights.

Because you are redeemed, you will start living a life unlike anything you knew before, and unlike anything you could ever imagine or think before you are *kept by the power*!

CHAPTER TEN

Keeping Me From Every Evil Work

Many years ago I found a cartoon in a magazine that deeply impressed me. It illustrated Pastor Jones in the corner of a room with his head in his hands. His wife and little newborn baby had their hands on their foreheads as well. The caption below said, "This is what Pastor Jones' family looks like when they decide not to talk about church."

When you are being kept by God and dwell in His promises, you do not need to try to keep yourself because Somebody is keeping you!

You don't have to try to make yourself joyful because Somebody is giving you the joy of the Lord.

You don't have to try to make yourself clean because Somebody is on the inside of you with a regeneration station regenerating you!

You do not need to try and make yourself righteous because you can declare, "In God I'm righteous. I'm kept by His promises. He keeps me at the level of His promises. My job is to know I'm not keeping myself because He keeps me where I am, being who I am, at the level of where I am."

He keeps you at the level of the desire of His promise.

He Keeps Me at the Level of His Peace

He keeps you at the level of His peace. If you are kept at the level of His peace, you will walk in Isaiah 26:3 which promises, *"Thou wilt keep him in perfect peace..."*

Do you see it? Not just peace, but *perfect* peace.

What is perfect peace?

Perfect peace is a constant peace, one that transcends your thinking. Perfect peace is a peace that is not subject to anything. It is not ruled by the flesh or decided by circumstance. It is not determined by whether you do or do not have money, whether you have or do not have food. God's goodness and His mercy determine your blessings.

Get Yourself a "Constant"

I was on the phone with someone recently and I told him, "Listen, you've got to have you a constant in your life."

"Bishop, what do you mean?" he asked.

"You've got to have something in your life that stays the same when everything else is different," I replied, "even if it's just an understanding that God is good."

Wake up in the morning and declare, "God is good."

In the afternoon reaffirm, "God is good." In the evening, boldly say, "God is good."

If you do not understand anything else in this book, get yourself a constant, because when everything else is bad you can look at everybody else and say, "God is good."

As you reaffirm your constant, Isaiah 26:3 promises, *"Thou wilt keep him in perfect peace..."*

He will keep you, surround you, garrison you in peace. The condition is *"whose mind is stayed on thee."*

I love the way the Amplified Bible phrases this statement:

> *You will guard him and keep him in perfect and constant peace whose mind [both its inclination and its character] is stayed on You because he commits himself to You, leans on You, and hopes confidently in You.*

LEAN ON THE WALL!

"Lord, thank You for keeping me in perfect, constant, unswerving, unsullied peace."

Why is He doing this?

Because you are committing yourself to Him; you are leaning on Him; you are hoping confidently in Him. You can know with assurance that God will keep you because He is the wall.

Regardless of what's going on in your life, remember, He is the wall you can lean on!

Yes, there will be times when you feel tired and do not want to stand. Sometimes you're going to feel like life is just too overwhelming. That is when you need to find the wall and lean on it hard! The strength of the wall is not contingent upon the amount of strength you possess.

We have all tried to walk in faith, but we've ended up walking through the flesh. We've tried to walk in the Spirit, but we frequently revert to the flesh to do our walking.

We say, "I am walking in the Spirit, I am walking by faith," but we keep throwing all of our do's, our don'ts, our rights, our wrongs, our points, and our techniques before God when He really only needs to hear a simple, three-word sentence. "Lord, help me!" If we can get those three words out of our mouths, then we're walking by faith.

There was a little song I used to sing in youth camp years ago which had three memorable lines. It said:

"There's somebody bigger than you and I. You make the stars that shine in the sky. Somebody bigger than you and I."

These words may be simple, but the meaning is clear: He's bigger than I am, and I can ultimately trust Him.

Deliverance From Every Evil

He keeps me at the level of His peace. The word "keep" means "to surround, to garrison, to build a force or a wall around". 2 Timothy 4:18 says: *"And the Lord shall deliver me from every evil work and will preserve me. . ."* The word "deliver" here is the same Greek word as for "keep."

Chapter Ten: Keeping Me From Every Evil Work

If the Lord is going to deliver you from every evil work, then He shall keep you at the level which this Scripture promises, *"from every evil work, and will preserve me."*

1 Peter 1:5 reminds us that the "inheritance inncorrruptible" is reserved for you and me. Verse 18 continues,

And the Lord shall deliver me from every evil work, and will preserve me unto his heavenly kingdom: to whom be glory for ever and ever. Amen.

You might say, "Wait a minute, Bishop. Are you saying that in all the things I go through, He is keeping me from every evil work?"

That's exactly what I'm saying.

"Well, then what does God call evil?"

Evil is anything that is bad.

If you can find out what God calls evil, then you can know what He's keeping you from. The phrase "every evil work" means "any apparent or literal form of decline." If "decline" means "going down," then God calls evil any apparent or literal form of going down.

If I get one percent less than the highest level of blessing, God says it is evil. If I get one day less of health, one dime less in the employment line, God says it's evil. If I have one level less than perfect peace, God calls it evil.

Do not be discouraged. God has promised that He is keeping you and delivering you from every evil work.

You are delivered! You are delivered from every apparent and literal form of going down.

As I meditated on that amazing promise of God, I thought about what David meant when he said in the Book of Psalms, *"If I make my bed in hell, You'll find me there."* That passage essentially means, "Lord, if I trip up or fall over, You are coming after me because it is an apparent and literal form of decline. Lord, any type of smoke that dims my vision and starts me plummeting, I know that you will not allow that (evil) to happen in my life."

The moment that decline begins, the very second the decline starts happening, He begins to put His blood, His power into that situation. You see, the Word says you are *kept by the power*.

The moment God sees decline, the very power that He used to raise Jesus from the dead, the very power He used to create the heavens and the earth, the very power that He uses to wake you up in the morning, the very power that causes every day to start, is the power He brings back to you.

He brings you back to His level of peace, victory and triumph! He puts power up under you and pushes you back up so that you don't go down. 2 Timothy 4:18 says he has *"delivered you from all manner of evil work."* The word "all" means "every, the whole, all manner of, all means of."

HE WILL NOT ALLOW DECLINE!

God shows us yet another representation of who He is to you. "I am your Daddy. I am your Papa, and will not

Chapter Ten: Keeping Me From Every Evil Work

allow decline to take place in you. I'm your El Shaddai, the all-breasted One, and you can only get life from Me-the One on the inside of you Who is keeping you. I won't let you decline. I won't let you go back. I won't let you fall down."

Let this sink into your spirit. Take the time in your daily prayer life to honor Him who keeps you from falling, who keeps you from declining, who keeps you from making one little degree of change downward.

But you say, "Bishop, you don't understand. I have real problems in my life." According to Him you don't. According to Him you're *kept by the power*. You may think you're kept by your actions, but you're only kept by His power. As long as you know you're *kept by the power*, you will be kept and maintained at the level of His peace.

"But Bishop, how can I be kept at the level of His peace today when I don't even have the money to pay my basic bills?"

The bills don't determine your peace; the phone company doesn't determine your peace; the doorbell doesn't determine your peace. Your peace is determined by keeping your mind stayed upon Him!

Now, this next revelation might shock you.

Whether you have ever thought about God or acknowledged His presence, He's still inside of you, willing to give you peace. You're kept by the power and are, therefore, free from all decline.

My Normally Expected Level

I began to examine this subject from various old

texts, old dictionaries and old writings, some of which are out of print today. One writer said, "Decline means any slope, any deviation, any descent, any slide from the normally expected level." God says you are preserved from any slide, any slope or deviation from the normally expected level.

"Well, then, Bishop, what is the normally expected level?"

2 Corinthians 2:14 says, *"Now thanks be to God which always causeth us to triumph in Christ."*

The Amplified Bible reads,

> *Who in Christ always leads us in triumph [as trophies of Christ's victory]. Now thanks be unto God, which always causeth us to triumph in Christ, and maketh manifest the savour of his knowledge by us in every place.*

"Did He say 'every place'? Even when somebody cuts me off on the road?" Yes, because He makes manifest the savor of the aroma of His knowledge in you.

"What do you mean, Bishop?"

He determines how He smells through you. You want to know how God smells?

God's Sweet-Smelling Aroma

I was at a perfumery in New Orleans, and a young lady came up to me. She observed that I choose colognes the same way I choose giftings in God. I believe if you pray over the right thing to put on your body, you can get somebody saved. I really believe that.

Chapter Ten: Keeping Me From Every Evil Work

Well, the saleswoman said, "Have you ever heard of the cologne called Eau de Animal?" It just so happened that on that particular day I had showered with my Eau Animal body shampoo. I had put a little suds in my hair with the *Eau de Animal*.

I replied, "Have you ever smelled Eau de Animal? Come here." I put some on me and had her smell the cologne. I then said, "That's how *Eau de Animal* is supposed to smell. I don't care how it smells in the bottle, this is how it's really supposed to smell when it is on the person."

God is saying, "I don't care what you read off the bottle, the real smell of Me comes from you. When you get up in the morning walking in victory with Me, whenever hell tries to come against you, and you say 'No', this is how I smell."

God makes manifest (reveals) how He smells through you, because He keeps you, He surrounds you, preserves you, and delivers you from every evil work. When you are on the highway, freeway or interstate, if there is any slope, any deviation or any decline, He delivers you from it. He restores you to your normally expected level so that you can always triumph in Christ Jesus.

Always.

A Truth Higher Than Reality

Stop letting decline be the norm in your life.

Start identifying and recognizing every slope.

Why does it have to be a slope where things are sliding all over? Any deviation from the norm, any change, even a fingernail's worth of deviation means that God calls it "every evil work."

If you discover one day less than the day you are living now; if you find a tomorrow less than today...

Don't allow it.

Pray this way.

"God, I thank You that You have delivered me." This simple prayer will stop those horrible mood swings we all sometimes find ourselves in. Even a woman's menstrual cycle has nothing to do with her mood. It is just a license to let the devil in.

"But Bishop, are you really saying that that's not real?"

No, a monthly mood swing is real, but you have a truth that is higher than that reality. You have a higher reality available to you, and your reality of praise and peace is higher than your reality of the time of the month. Ladies, don't you dare categorize and compartmentalize a few days a month as your personal hell. Don't allow others to run from you because once a month you suddenly grow horns and claws. Don't you dare!

And that principle applies for the men as well. It seems that every 48 hours we find our tails stuck between our legs, and we can't figure out whether we are supposed to be grownups or children, whether we are supposed to be heads of our homes or the kids of the house. Men, don't you dare compartmentalize every 48 hours or a weekend a month to give the devil a chance!

You are kept from every evil work!

Chapter Ten: Keeping Me From Every Evil Work

You say, "Bishop, I don't believe that?"

Get out your health book. It will tell you that men go through a cycle similar to a woman's menstrual cycle every 48 hours; so men, get yourself some spiritual Midol. You are kept from every evil work also. You are kept from any slope, any slide, any slant and any deviation.

He has called it evil so you can see that He's delivered you from every evil work of the enemy. He does not want you to just identify it as evil, He wants you to understand that you are delivered from evil.

More Than Conquerors

When you are under trying circumstances, when you don't have enough food for groceries this week, or are feeling down and blue, when you don't understand why your child is acting the way he is, say the first word that is found in Romans 8:37: *"No"*.

The rest of this encouraging passage reads, *"No, in all these things we are more than conquerors. . ."* This is the answer for all those things that come upon you, for all the evil that tries to rob you of the riches God has prepared for you. In all these things, *"we are more than conquerors."*

Notice, He didn't say conquerors, He said "more than conquerors." For years I wanted to know, "Why in the world did He say 'more.'" He said "more" because if you are a conqueror, you have to fight, but if you are more than a conqueror, Somebody else gives you the victory. If you are just a conqueror, you only get what you fight for.

It's called conquest. Conquest is the art and act of something conquerors get. But God didn't say "You are a conqueror." He said, "You are more than a conqueror." If you are more than one, bless God, you don't have to fight for victory. The battle belongs to Him, but the victory is yours.

He keeps you from all decline. In all these things, you are more than a conqueror *"through him who loved us."* Not just a conqueror, but more than a conqueror!

Chapter Eleven

The Inheritance That Awaits You

We have an inheritance that is incorruptible, undefiled, and that fadeth not away. 1 Peter 4-5 tells us,

> *To an inheritance incorruptible, and undefiled, and that fadeth not away, reserved in heaven for you, Who are kept by the power of God through faith unto salvation ready to be revealed in the last time.*

The Amplified Bible says we have an inheritance that is "imperishable, unsullied, and unfading." Of course, we learned that not only is it all those things, it is also reserved in heaven for us.

I want you to notice that verse 5 says,

> *Who are kept by the power of God through faith unto salvation ready to be revealed in the last time.*

The blessing is reserved for you.

You are reserved for it.

You have your own set of bodyguards who have been commissioned by God to make sure you get the blessing. You can't miss it. The blessing doesn't just mean something monetary or something that is physical. It means whatever your destiny is supposed to produce.

What God Promises, He Guarantees

"But you don't understand, Bishop," you might say, "I've made wrong decisions."

God will take your wrong decisions and redeem them, bringing you to right decisions if you let Him keep you. It doesn't matter if on the way to your future you have made some decisions that did not work out just right. He is still keeping you. In the middle of those wrong decisions, He is going to work it out for your good. God's not finished with you yet.

"Inheritance" means "an heirship." When a person is an heir, they are going to receive something that someone has for them. An heirship literally means "to have a promised possession." If you have a promised possession, it is also guaranteed.

Whatever God promises He also guarantees.

Reading from Genesis through Revelation is nothing more than reading God's simple, solitary promise to you. Because it is His promise, it is also His guarantee: there is nothing that can keep you from getting it. It is an inheritance to you.

You say, "But I thought that somebody has to die before I get an inheritance."

You're absolutely right. Jesus did die. A last will and

Chapter Eleven: The Inheritance That Awaits You

testament is activated when somebody dies. But there is no stipulation in the contract that says when you die, you cannot come back from the dead. That's just what Jesus did. When He died, everything that belonged to Him was transferred to me. But on the third day, the Bible says that Jesus Christ rose from the dead.

By getting up out of the grave, Jesus came back to make sure that not only do you have His promise and His will, but also the Holy Spirit to orchestrate His will. You have received the Holy Spirit to show you how to receive His power. And, you are also being kept by His power so that you do not miss it.

ENTRUSTED TO GOD'S PROTECTION

The word "inheritance" not only means "a promised possession," but it also means "to get my portion." In Acts 20:32, Paul is getting ready to leave and makes a statement to his pastors. He says in verse 28,

> *Take heed therefore unto yourselves, and to all the flock, over which the Holy Ghost hath made you overseers, to feed the church of God, which he hath purchased with his own blood.*

Paul essentially said that the Church of God has been purchased with the blood of Jesus. He goes on to say in verse 29, *"After my departing shall grievous wolves enter in among you."*

They are going to enter in.

Verse 30 continues, *"Also of your own selves shall men arise, speaking perverse things,"* which means that if you do not hold on to the Truth, there is a tendency for perverse things to rise up from within.

A bit farther in verse 31 he warns,

Therefore watch, and remember, that by the space of three years I ceased not to warn every one night and day. And now, brethren, I commend you to God.

"*I deposit you,*" the Amplified Bible says, "*in His charge, entrusting you to His protection and care.*"

When Paul said, "*I commend you to God,*" He was saying, "I am entrusting you to be *kept by the power.*" If you are *kept by the power*, you can also be sure you know what it means to be entrusted in God's protection. He continues, saying, "...and to the word of his grace, which is able to build you up."

That same Word, the Word of God, that Word of victory, that Word of faith, is able to give you an inheritance amongst all of them who are sanctified.

When you are under this Word, it is able to give you your inheritance, and establish your mindset so you are able to receive your promised possession.

This is why, when you hear people say, "When you miss a church service, it's like missing the best part of a movie", they mean it is hard to miss because you are lacking your promised possession.

Christina Onassis' Inheritance

If you have an inheritance, then your challenge is to listen, to learn, to receive, to receive the education, to receive all the information you can get concerning that inheritance.

Chapter Eleven: The Inheritance That Awaits You

The Word of God essentially says that as long as a child remains at a child's age, even though he is an heir, he will never reap the benefits of his heirship.

Christina Onassis was recently in the news because when she turned eighteen, she received her family inheritance of well over a billion dollars. That's a pretty hefty little gift for one's birthday.

Christina was a billionaire before she turned eighteen, but her parents could not put her billions into her hands before the age of eighteen.

For the last eighteen years, they have been teaching, training and educating her on how to be a billionaire, how to walk in the inheritance that has been waiting for her.

Trained for Victory

You have an inheritance that is much more than a billion dollars. You have an eternal fortune in the heavens. Your heritage is worth more than Fort Knox could give you, and more than any check that could be written to you.

Because of this truth, you have to be trained to reign, trained to be victorious, and trained to have the right mindset so you can walk in the benefit of your promised possession. It does not do any good to have all of His wealth if you do not know what to do with it.

Who do you think was helping Christina spend her money the first seventeen years of her life? With both of her parents dead, she had tutors and governors. Can you imagine? The lady of the house was a child. The salary of everyone who served her came out of her pocket, but no one was able to give her what was hers until she turned eighteen. She will receive the second half of her money when she turns twenty-one. They are now spacing the rest of the money due her to see if the training was proper and if she can prove trustworthy and responsible with what has already been given to her.

Scripture says all things are yours.

But, as with everything He does, God does not want you to forsake the assembling of yourselves together in church. The Amplified Bible says not to refuse your church meetings because when you receive the proper instruction, you will know how to handle your billions.

You may ask, "Am I supposed to have it all now?"

No.

You are supposed to know what to do with what you have as it is coming to you. As you demonstrate good stewardship, He will flow more into your life.

You frequently hear the "rags to riches" stories of people winning the lottery or the Publisher's Clearinghouse Sweepstakes. The sad part about these events is that many of the winners end up squandering all of their winnings within a year because they have not been trained to handle their sudden wealth.

That is why it is so important for us to be trained about how to handle money and invest. If you personally do not want to invest, then pay someone else to do it for you, or put your money aside in an appreciating account, then leave it alone.

Chapter Eleven: The Inheritance That Awaits You

TRAIN UP YOUR CHILDREN FOR THEIR INHERITANCE

Many Christians need to learn that old four-letter word, "S-A-V-E".

Some would say, "The market is too volatile right now. It's too risky; I don't want to get involved in that."

Saving is not volatile or risky. The market is a little slower right now, but doing something with your money is better than doing nothing.

If you have a child, on a monthly basis put money into his or her savings account. Do all you can to help your children and your children's children become wealthy. To enable your child or grandchild to become a millionaire, it has been said that you only need to deposit $50 every month from their ages of 7 to 25.

Do the math; that may be true.

Time is passing, so be sure you train your child.

Scripture says,

> *A good man leaveth an inheritance to his children's children;*
>
> (Proverbs 13:22)

Why?

Because they have all been trained on how to act with an inheritance.

We need to be raising up our level of how we should be acting with increase so that our kids do not need to take a crash course on how to deal with money.

Your inheritance includes your spiritual life, your health, your wealth, your mental stability, peace of mind and perpetual increase. That means long after you are gone, your bloodline will still be walking in increase and abundance.

Always remember that the most important thing you will ever do in God is to learn how to operate at the highest height of what He's already done. He wants you to be able to know how to possess the promised blessing.

Inheritance Is a Matter of Birth

God says His Word is able to give you an inheritance among all whom are sanctified. Another part of the definition of "inheritance" is "one who is a sharer by lot."

In Ephesians 1 we find what we generally call the Ephesians prayer, which starts off by Paul praying in verse 17,

> *That the God of our Lord Jesus Christ, the Father of glory, may give unto you the spirit of wisdom and revelation in the knowledge of him.*

Do you understand what will happen to you if you have the revelation and the knowledge of Him?

> *The eyes of your understanding being enlightened; that ye may know what is the hope of his calling, and what the riches of the glory of his inheritance in the saints.*

The Amplified Bible says that I many know "how rich is His glorious inheritance in the saints." In other words, God has given a glorious promised possession to those who are set apart by Him!

Chapter Eleven: The Inheritance That Awaits You

If you have an inheritance, no one can take it from you. Your inheritance will appear in your spiritual life: health, wealth, mental stability, peace of mind and perpetual increase. You, your seed, and your seed's seed will be blessed.

Notice that this inheritance has already been promised. This inheritance, by virtue of 1 Peter, is not only promised, but it is sitting in the heavens right now waiting for you. It is not going to be put there afresh, it is not going to be put there anew, it is already there waiting for you.

In fact, whenever a child is born into a family, that child doesn't have to have a new inheritance. That child becomes a recipient of the same inheritance his parents have.

From the time when Christina Onassis was born into this world, she was already a billionaire, an inheritor of the blessings of her family. Of course, she did not know it at the time, nor did she understand that she could eventually spend it. Christina was called the richest child in the world because, as an infant, all of her family's wealth belonged to her.

Likewise, before you are able to understand what God has done for you, His inheritance is yours. No matter what bad things you have done or will do in life, you cannot lose your inheritance.

"But Bishop, what if I do something that is extremely bad? Is it still mine?"

When we do not understand what belongs to us, we still have a tendency to mess up things. But, your inheritance is still yours because it is a matter of birth, not action.

You are born into your blessing.

Inheritance Cannot Be Earned

Your inheritance is a matter of position, not plea.

It is a matter of birth, not behavior.

Receiving your inheritance is a matter of attitude, not action. You see, you have an inheritance whether you act like you have one or not.

If you feel like you have to earn your inheritance, it's not an inheritance yet. People who understand that they have an inheritance act similarly. You don't see the children of wealthy people acting like they have to earn their wealth. They walk and function in it. In the early 1900s, the Rockefeller children were groomed to take over their father's business. In fact, they were not allowed to leave the premises of the estate until they were almost adults.

You say, "Bishop, but wouldn't that hurt them?"

No. Did you hear what their last name was? The Rockefellers owned an Olympic-sized swimming pool, full-size tennis courts, and even had a bowling alley at the mansion. Everything the children might have wanted to do away from the house, their smart Daddy built within their house.

Their training, tutelage, education and intellectualism was spawned and sharpened at their home. When the day came to leave the house and run the business, they were fully trained.

The comedy movie "Richie Rich" contains the same principles. In one scene, the children are sitting at

Chapter Eleven: The Inheritance That Awaits You

school at their big executive desks faxing notes to each other. They are learning how to function and be successful.

Likewise, God's people must receive the Word of the Lord and learn how to walk powerfully in victory and triumph.

It is a matter of attitude, not action. If you keep your attitude right, it will determine your attitude in God. It's what you think of a thing that will determine how high you go in it. It's not your behavior, it's your birth. Your name will be "Believer" when you receive Jesus whether you act like one or not.

A Matter of Position

What position are you in?

I am in Christ.

You are in Christ.

Because you are in Christ, you are out of the world and in His Kingdom. Being in the Kingdom means you're in abundance, you're out of lack.

Without an inheritance?

Never!

If you are an individual with an inheritance, you cannot ever be without one because you received it at birth. You were born into it. How can you lose it? It cannot happen.

Isn't it true that on the very day you were saved you were told that "When you die you're going to live forever?" Eternal life became yours the very second you accepted Christ. "Death" means "to be separated from God." "Eternal life" means "to be connected to Him forevermore." The wealth of your inheritance became yours the very moment you accepted Christ into your heart.

I don't care if you came to Jesus with a bag of food stamps; He said "You now have an inheritance."

If you were on death row with the electrodes stuck on your head and in your hands, and you cried out, "Lord, save me," you are more free at that very moment than the man pulling the switch.

It is a matter of birth.

As believers we spend all our time trying to get what is already ours. It begins to be a work of vanity, a work of futility. We are working for things we already have and are struggling to get something that already belongs to us. We are fighting to have what we already possess.

On the worst day of your life, you will still have an inheritance. On the devil's best day, he could never, ever have what you have. The devil may have a good day, but he still has no inheritance. You may have a day where you don't even feel that you are saved, but it is not about your feelings; your inheritance is intact.

God says "You are good, and I love you."

Married couples learn quickly that marriage is not about feeling the love. Some of us have many of those days where we do not "feel" the love. But, is not about the feelings of love, it is about commitment. We subscribe to commitment, we do not subscribe to a feeling; feelings are not permanent.

Chapter Eleven: The Inheritance That Awaits You

It is the same way with your inheritance. Whether you feel like you deserve it or not, whether you act like you have it or not, it is a matter of your position and birth.

Chapter Twelve

Trained for Your Inheritance

We need to be trained to know what to do with our inheritance. Proverbs 24:3-4, my favorite Scripture, tells us,

> *Through wisdom is an house builded; and by understanding it is established: And by knowledge shall the chambers be filled with all precious and pleasant riches.*

The Amplified Bible says,

> *Through skillful and godly Wisdom is a house (a life, a home, a family) built, and by understanding it is established [on a sound and good foundation], And by knowledge shall its chambers [of every area] be filled with all precious and pleasant riches.*

The Living Bible, using yet a third comparison, says,

> *A house is built by wisdom and becomes strong through good sense. Through knowledge its rooms*

are filled with all sorts of precious riches and valuables.

Any enterprise is meant to be funded through wise planning. It becomes strong through common sense, and it will profit wonderfully by keeping abreast of all the facts.

Common sense means practical judgment. You don't take a ten-foot drop off an eight-foot pier. You don't take a high dive into three feet of water. You study where you are going to jump. That practical insight will help you walk in wisdom for the rest of your life.

WEALTH IS YOURS

Believe in God to be able to have and walk in abundance and prosperity. Your inheritance is in the area of your Father's wealth.

If you believe God is able to operate in your inheritance concerning wealth, you need to understand and see what God says about it. You must find out what God says about your inheritance concerning perpetual, generational blessing and covering.

If God said to you, "This is your year of 24-hour receiving, the year of harvest, the year of multiplication," you would start taking inventory of things you need to be multiplied, and start discarding off the stuff you do not want to be multiplied.

There must be some things in your life that you do not want to be multiplied. For example, you do not want trouble multiplied, or your bills multiplied.

If this is the year of your multiplication, you want to

Chapter Twelve: Trained for Your Inheritance

specify what you want multiplied. You need to gather some information about your inheritance so that you will be able to flow.

Remember, you don't have to receive your inheritance, you already received it when you were born in Christ. 2 Corinthians 5:17 tells you precisely when you received your inheritance:

> *Therefore if any man be in Christ, he is a new creature: old things are passed away; behold, all things are become new.*

The next verse through verse 19 says,

> *And all things are of God, who hath reconciled us to himself by Jesus Christ, and hath given to us the ministry of reconciliation; To wit, that God was in Christ, reconciling the world unto himself, not imputing their trespasses unto them; and hath committed unto us the word of reconciliation.*

The Amplified Bible says,

> *Therefore if any person is [ingrafted] in Christ (the Messiah) he is a new creation (a new creature altogether); the old [previous moral and spiritual condition] has passed away. Behold, the fresh and new has come!*

The fresh you has come; the new you has come. He says, "*But all things are from God, Who, through Jesus Christ, reconciled us to Himself.*" The very moment you received Jesus into your life, your old spiritual condition, your old moral condition, your old receiving capacity died. The way you would reason things, the way you would receive things, all died.

THE PROMISES OF YOUR NEW CONDITION

When you receive, you receive from a new spiritual condition, a new moral center. Even the way you receive is totally different. If you are a new being who never existed before, behold, when the fresh and new come, your whole condition is new because you are new...you have a new name, a new covering, and a new Father.

Those things are a part of your inheritance because once you have received Him, you have been positionally shifted under a new heading. This heading then begins to bring you to a new outcome. If there were promises under your old spiritual and moral condition, there are promises under your new spiritual and moral condition.

What were the promises under the old?

The promises under the old were that your outward and inward man would decay because your inward man did not know God. According to Ephesians 2:1, you and I by nature were the children of wrath. In other words, if you had tried to do good, you may have done some moral deeds but your moral condition was against God. You may have done some things that seemed spiritually right, but your spiritual condition was against God.

But then, when you received Jesus, you were by nature a child of obedience. Even on your worst day, your nature still slipped out of the bowels of the old and into the portal of the new. On your best day while you were in the world, you may have been able to feel the presence of God, but you were still separated from Him. You had no inheritance from Him; your inheritance was of the devil.

Now that you have the nature of God, you have God's

Chapter Twelve: Trained for Your Inheritance

inheritance, which means on your worst day in God, on the day when you can't tell your head from your rear end, you still have an inheritance. On the day when you say, "Bishop, I haven't even had time to pray today," you still have an inheritance.

I am not trying to promote a lack of prayer. My point is simply that it is not about works, it is not about all the things you think you can do. There are not enough things you can do to make yourself good enough for God to bless you.

You have an inheritance in spite of yourself!

Just keep getting out of the way of you. That generally is the reason why we miss what we are supposed to have — we keep getting in the way of ourselves.

OUR PROMISED POSSESSIONS ARE IN THE HEAVENLY REALM

Ephesians 1:3 says,

> *Blessed be the God and Father of our Lord Jesus Christ, who hath blessed us with all spiritual blessings in heavenly places in Christ.*

If God gave us the right to rewrite this verse, here's what we could accurately say:

"Blessed be the God and Father of our Lord Jesus Christ, who hath given us a promised possession in heavenly places in Christ. These promised possessions have been given to us. They are in the heavenly realm."

They are not in the heavenly realm waiting for you to

die so you can receive them when you get to heaven. They are in the heavenly realm because God preserves them from Satan, the ruler of this world.

And because Satan is the god of this world, some things are subject to rust, corruption, inflation and deterioration, but the things God gives us that we put in the heavenly realm cannot be affected by rust. Moths can't eat it, rust can't corrupt it, thieves can't break through and steal it, and politicians can't cheat you out of what is yours.

"But, Bishop, how can I get to it," you ask," "if it's in the heavenly realm?"

Just like you have deposit slips and withdrawal slips for your bank, so too you have the exact same thing for your inheritance. Notice what verses 3-5 say:

He hath blessed us with all spiritual blessings in heavenly places in Christ: According as he hath chosen us in him before the foundation of the world, that we should be holy and without blame before him in love, predestined us unto the adoption of children by Jesus Christ to himself, according to the good pleasure of his will.

Verse 6 continues, *"He hath made us accepted in the beloved."*

If you are one who spends days and months in depression, meditate on this verse daily and you will forget about depression. You can't be both rejected and accepted at the same time.

Verse 7, *"In whom we have redemption through his blood, the forgiveness of sins, according to the riches of his grace"* means you have been bought by the blood.

Chapter Twelve: Trained for Your Inheritance

Notice verse 8 in the King James Version demonstrates how much He lavishes upon us, "*Wherein he hath abounded toward us in all wisdom and prudence.*" The Amplified Bible reads, "*Which He lavished upon us in every kind of wisdom and understanding.*"

Verse 9 continues that He has "*made known unto us the mystery of his will, according to his good pleasure which he hath purposed in himself.*"

Verse 10 reads,

That in the dispensation of the fullness of times he might gather together in one all things in Christ, both which are in heaven, and which are on earth; even in him.

He has gathered all things in Christ.

Next, verse 11 says,

In whom also we have obtained an inheritance, being predestinated according to the purpose of him who worketh all things after the counsel of his own will.

"What in the world is He saying to us, Bishop?"

In verse 10, He gathered together in one all things-- all things, every good thing, every perfect thing, every blessed thing, every beneficial thing, everything that is of advantage, everything that gets you over and keeps you from going under.

He has given you all those things.

He Has Blessed Us With All Spiritual Blessings

The moment I accepted Christ, I received whatever was in Christ. I received my inheritance. He didn't hide my inheritance in a back room somewhere in heaven, He put my inheritance in heavenly places in Christ.

But I came out of darkness and got into the light.

"How, Bishop?"

By getting into the light in Christ. As long as I remain in Christ, that is where my inheritance will be. I can't be in Christ and out of my blessing.

Some believers have been cheated out of their blessings because, even though they have received a spiritual work called salvation, they have understood it purely in a natural sense.

If you receive it and understand it spiritually, you will understand that you don't have to work for it.

If you've got to work for it, there are going to be some days when you are going to get different levels of blessings. But if you will understand He has blessed you with all spiritual blessings in heavenly places in Christ, then you will know He has gathered together in one place in Christ all things.

Verse 11 says,

In whom also we have obtained an inheritance, being predestinated according to the purpose of him who worketh all things after the counsel of his own will.

Chapter Twelve: Trained for Your Inheritance

We know the prefix "pre" means "before." The word "destined" means "the conclusion." In other words, God wrote your conclusion before He wrote your beginning! He wants you to run on ahead and see what the end is going to be.

Long before you had sense enough to come to Jesus, your inheritance was hidden in Christ. Men, while you and I were busy chasing anything but God, our inheritances were hidden in Christ. God was waiting on a time, waiting on a special moment.

MARKED WITH HIS LOVING KINDNESS

The Bible says "with His lovingkindness" He draws you in. Your inheritance is already marked with His loving kindness. The most precious things you could ever want to love in your whole life He has predestined to be eternally yours.

But, you say, "Is it really tailor-made for me?"

You bet it is!

Salvation is the most corporate thing with a most individual touch. When you receive Him, you are receiving your inheritance.

He's predestined us according to "the purpose of him who worketh all things after the counsel of his own will." The words "saint of God" and "depression" should never be in the same sentence — defeat and victory cannot walk together. God has invested everything that makes you able to praise Him in Jesus Christ. He's invested it all in Jesus.

What do you think God means when He says you are "hidden" with Him?

When you were hidden in Him, He pulled out His inheritance package for you that included all the wonderful things that would bring you to a place of peace, joy and fulfillment. It's all the things He promises in verse 12 so that...

We should be to the praise of his glory, who first trusted in Christ.

Those of us who received our inheritance shall be to His praise and glory. In other words, when we first trusted in Him, we found out very quickly that He didn't just want to save us, He didn't just want to give us fire insurance to keep us out of hell, He kept us out of the hell on this earth. He is giving us a place where we can escape the corruption that is in the world.

That inheritance will cause you to praise Him, to glorify Him and bless Him. You can't lose it. You can't miss it because it is reserved in Christ in the heavenly places for you. You can be blind in one eye and can't see out of the other and still get this inheritance. You can make wise choices one day and be stupid the rest of the week and still receive it.

This is not the kind of blessing that is reserved for only one nationality, nor is it reserved just for preachers or for the scholarly. In fact, I would venture to say that the more scholarly we are, the more we will miss this blessing. This isn't the kind of stuff that God lays out for scholars; He lays it out for the simple. The simpler we can become, the more we will be able to receive what He has for us.

Chapter Twelve: Trained for Your Inheritance

GOD ADDS A GUARANTEE

Ephesians 1:13 tells us,

In whom ye also trusted, after that ye heard the word of truth, the gospel of your salvation: in whom also after that ye believed, ye were sealed with that holy Spirit of promise.

After you believe, you are a sealed believer.

"*And have believed in and adhered to and relied on Him,*" the Amplified Bible says, "[You] *were stamped with the seal of the long-promised Holy Spirit.*"

When a man says those infamous words, "Will you marry me?", they are just words until he adds a guarantee. The word "marriage" implies a lifetime commitment. The man is to be the woman's lifetime provider. He must allow God to empower him and to be God's personal representative to take good care of his wife. God will deputize him and let the man have the ministry of being what God would be if He lived on this earth.

Now the woman would say, "That sounds good, but that's not enough, Baby. I need something more; I need a guarantee, an earnest note, a security deposit. I need a trust. I need to know that you "*ain't*" just giving me some empty words that are going to go away tomorrow when you digest your last meal. Show me something that's going to cut through the temporal and begin to cut down into the eternal. I want to know you're going to put your money where your mouth is."

The Ultimate Security Deposit

The very powerful Greek word "arrabon" means "the security deposit," the proof that everything a person is saying is true; they will do what they say they will do.

Here's the proof of it.

The stone does not come in the wedding band, it is usually found in the engagement ring. The wedding is nothing more than the tollgate to get started doing everything you said you were going to do. If the facts were known, and the truth was told, it's the engagement that proves you are going to be what you are going to be. If enough women had the basic common sense to watch the man during the engagement period, and NOT get wrapped up in fantasy, many of them would not be stupid enough to let that man get them to the altar. The engagement is the security deposit, the down payment.

Baby, if he can't be what he needs to be during the engagement, he is not going to be what he needs to be after the wedding. If you are arguing and disagreeing throughout your entire engagement period, God is telling you something. This may not be Prince Charming!

And God is telling you that when you become a believer, you are hidden in Christ. He gave you an eternal inheritance, a promised possession. Just as the bride needs more than a few words as a commitment, Jesus says, "Let me put on your finger the security deposit called the Holy Spirit of promise. I'm going to give you an earnest, a down payment, a deposit of what I'm going to be for you.

"Your life in Christ with the Holy Ghost is the way things are going to be always. I'm giving you just a little

Chapter Twelve: Trained for Your Inheritance

taste, an engagement, via the Holy Spirit, of what your inheritance is all about."

That is why when the wedding comes along, it is only a band that is given during the wedding. Because if things ever get a little sour after the "I do's", the wife can look down at the stone in her engagement ring and have peace fill her heart. The wedding band is just the crossing over, but the engagement ring signifies the groom's promises and commitment.

THE GIFT OF THE HOLY GHOST

God gave you the Holy Ghost as His promise of the inheritance He has planned for you.

"And what did this Spirit of God do, Bishop?"

The Spirit of God represents Him on earth. John 16 essentially says, "He will lead me and guide me into all truth. He will show me things to come. He will remind me of what things Jesus said. He's going to be a generator on the inside of me."

That's the engagement. If that's the engagement, I can't imagine what the wedding night will be like!

"What's the wedding night going to be like if the Holy Ghost is my engagement," you ask?

You're sealed with the Holy Spirit of promise. Verse 14 says, *"which is the earnest. . ."* The Amplified Bible says *"guaranteed of our inheritance until the redemption of the purchased possession, unto the praise of his glory."* This means that [Spirit] is the guarantee of our inheritance [the firstfruits, the pledge and foretaste, the down payment on our heritage], in anticipation of its full redemption and our acquiring [complete] possession of it—to the praise of His glory.

You can expect your full redemption because you have the firstfruits, the Holy Ghost.

You have the pledge. You are in full anticipation that things will work out for you.

Acts 1:8 tells us, *"But ye shall receive power."* *"Power"* means *"ability."* We have a firstfruit in the down payment of the Holy Spirit of promise, which is His power.

Are you beginning to understand why you can receive all the blessings of God, your inheritance, and not miss it?

It is not about your behavior or your pleas.

1 Peter 1:5 did not say that *"You are kept by your behavior and ability."* It says you are *kept by the power.*

"What power, Bishop?"

But ye shall receive power, after that the Holy Ghost is come upon you.

The Holy Ghost is the down payment, the firstfruits of your inheritance.

You Are Presented Faultless

When you became a believer, He hid you in heavenly places with Him.

Old things are passed away; behold, all things are become new.

(2 Corinthians 5:17)

Chapter Twelve: Trained for Your Inheritance

All things are of God, who hath reconciled us to Himself by Jesus Christ.

Knowing that you have been bought by the blood, and are not in the world anymore, you are out of darkness and into His marvelous light.

You can stand and do not have to fall.

Now, unto Him who is able to keep us from falling and to present me faultless before the Presence of His glory with exceedingly great joy.
(Jude 1:24)

Just when you are getting ready to stumble, when you are about to fall over, when you are so tired that you can't go on anymore, the mighty power, the hand of the Holy Ghost, lifts you and stands you back up. Then by the blood of Jesus, He washes and cleanses you, presenting you as faultless before the presence of His glory.

You are cleansed by the blood.

You are redeemed in the blood and He keeps you under the blood. This is why John essentially says, "Now are you clean through the Word which is spoken unto you."

The Word is driven by the Spirit, and the Spirit is power, and the power is keeping you for your inheritance.

CHAPTER THIRTEEN

The Power of an Heir

In Proverbs 2:8 reads,

> *He keepeth the paths of judgment, and preserveth the way of his saints.*

The Amplified Bible says, "Yes, He preserves the way of His saints." One of the cross-referencing Scriptures listed in the Amplified Bible is Psalm 66:8 which begins to give us an insight on how He keeps us.

> *O bless our God, ye people, and make the voice of his praise to be heard: Which holdeth our soul in life, and suffereth not our feet to be moved.*

I don't care if you are in a grease pit, and crisis is just pushing you backward, His Word says He will not allow your feet to be moved.

I don't care if this is the last day, and you've got to have it all or everything is going to be taken, His Word says He suffered not our feet to be moved. Their deadline is not God's deadline.

> *For thou, O God, hast proved us: thou hast tried us, as silver is tried. Thou broughtest us into the net; thou laidst affliction upon our loins. Thou hast caused men to ride over our heads; we went through fire and through water but thou broughtest us out into a wealthy place.*

The wealthy place is one of the ways God is going to keep you in. Not only is He going to use the wealthy place to keep you, but He will use what happens to you in the wealthy place to hold your position.

Some may say, "What do you mean, Bishop?"

Your firstfruits emanate from the wealthy place and are sown into the good ground of God. You get an angel named "Shekinah" which means "the glorious power of God, the very power, the presence of God."

His power keeps you from falling.

Bishop, you mean to tell me that my firstfruits have something to do with me being kept by the power?"

Absolutely.

Notice that verse 13 says,

> *I will go into thy house with burnt offerings: I will pay thee my vows, Which my lips have uttered, and my mouth hath spoken, when I was in trouble.*

In other words, when you are in trouble, you begin to speak out, "Lord, I will bring You a seed. I'm not going to be moved by the lack of time. I'm not going to be moved by layoff threats. I'm going to bring You my vow. Use my faith and do not allow my feet to be moved."

Chapter Thirteen: The Power of an Heir

Your inheritance is a promised possession, an heirship.

TRAINING AN HEIR

Now I say, That the heir, as long as he is a child, differeth nothing from a servant, though he be lord of all.

(Galatians 4:1)

From the day a person becomes an heir, he becomes the sole possessor of the entire estate. Galatians 4:1 begins to outline how that process works.

In another chapter of this book, we saw how the young Onassis girl became a billionaire, and the sole possessor of the estate, when she turned 18. She was a billionaire long before that day; it was merely the control of that wealth which came to her when she turned 18.

You too are a multi-mega-billionaire many times over, but like Christina, the estate is not just turned over to you. You must first be trained. It says,

The heir, as long as he is a child, differeth nothing from a servant, though he be lord of all.

But notice verse 2 says,

But is under tutors and governors until the time appointed of the father.

God has placed you in a position where the Kingdom of God belongs to you, but God gives us apostles, prophets, evangelists, pastors and teachers for the perfecting, for the training of the saints.

For the perfecting of the saints, for the work of the ministry, for the edifying of the body of Christ: Till we all come in the unity of the faith, and of the knowledge of the Son of God, unto a perfect man, unto the measure of the stature of the fulness of Christ: That we henceforth be no more children, tossed to and fro, and carried about with every wind of doctrine, by the sleight of men, and cunning craftiness, whereby they lie in wait to deceive; But speaking the truth in love, may grow up into him in all things, which is the head, even Christ: From whom the whole body fitly joined together and compacted by that which every joint supplieth, according to the effectual working in the measure of every part, maketh increase of the body unto the edifying of itself in love.

(Ephesians 4:12-16)

God is saying that He provides the fivefold ministry gifts to train us on how to be equipped so we can know how to flow in our inheritance.

Your inheritance already belongs to you, but you still need to be trained in how to flow with it.

I strongly advocate that parents begin to teach their kids how to flow and function with wealth. If you don't begin to train them how to handle that little bit of change you give them, they will spend it like they have no understanding or respect of money. You watch your child. If that little bit of money you give them is always turned into candies, cookies, or name-brand shoes, they are outlining a pattern. You must start to show them how to respect wealth.

Your Heavenly Father owns the cattle on a thousand

Chapter Thirteen: The Power of an Heir

hills, and you are born into the inherited wealth that is in your bloodline.

- Heirship indicates your inheritance.
- Heirship indicates your name.
- Heirship indicates your identity.
- Heirship indicates your possession.

DRIVING OUT PREVIOUS TENANTS

The Word "heir" is the Greek word "Yaresh" which means "to occupy by driving out the previous tenant and taking possession in their place."

When you are an heir, you inherit everything that the previous tenant tried to possess. The "previous tenant" here is Satan, the god of this world. Because you are an heir, your possession is the earth and the fullness thereof.

You remember the story.

Once upon a time in the book of Genesis, a man named Adam was created in the image and likeness of God. God gave him possession of the earth. This man, through an act of high treason, took the possessions God gave him and turned the keys of the earth over to Satan. At that point, the earth had a lease on it. Satan became the landlord of the earth.

Man became a servant, a slave of the evil taskmaster. God outlined His recovery plan for man in Genesis 3:15 when He essentially said to Satan, "The day will come when someone will bruise your head." In other words, "Satan, Somebody is going to snatch from you what you think you've got. You think you have become the landlord of this property, but Somebody is coming to occupy the land again. Somebody is coming to evict you from the property. Somebody is coming to put your narrow behind out and take over the possession of the earth all over again. And, you won't be able to stop Him because those who are coming are born of Me."

If somebody is sent, they are on assignment.

If somebody is born of God, it is like God; they represent God Himself. They possess the same power, and the enemy cannot stop them.

The devil is not evicted by techniques but by the blood.

In the book of John, Jesus is called the "Only begotten Son."

> *For God so loved the world that He gave His only begotten Son.*
> (John 3:16)

That is the only place in God's Word where He is called the only begotten Son. After that time period, He is called the "first begotten Son" because He was no longer the only son of God. Jesus was the first, and now God is using His sons who have come after Jesus, made in His image and likeness, born just like Him.

God didn't just see Jesus brought back to life in hell. He watched you brought back to life as well. The enemy thought you died, but you were raised with Him.

You occupy by driving out a former tenant who does not want to go. I pray it gives you incredible encouragement as you understand your authority to move the enemy off the place he now possesses.

- Serve him an eviction notice!
- Seize control, and expel him!
- Bring him to poverty!

Your Incorruptible Inheritance

When Satan steals from you, he considers himself prosperous until you begin to turn the tables on him. When you understand that your inheritance is incorruptible, you are an heir, you can flow into your inheritance, even if you do not fully understand what is yours.

The young Christina didn't understand everything about being a billionaire, but she is one anyway. It is her money whether she fully understands it or not. It is her estate. She may not understand everything about where all the money goes, but she's still a billionaire because she was born into it. Even when she was a baby who couldn't speak articulately, she was a billionaire.

Likewise, even when you don't understand Genesis to Revelation, you still own the cattle on a thousand hills. The earth is still the Lord's, and you're still His child. And the fullness of the earth is the fullness of His children.

What God's got, you've got, because you are His child!

Understanding Your Name

To the degree that you understand your name, you will hold onto your victory. Understand there is no conquest or contest in a name. Once you possess a name, you never have to fight because the name is on you.

"So, then, Bishop, where does warfare come from?"

Warfare comes from you coming into the reality of your name. Regardless of what your name is, it is how long it takes you to understand what is inherent in that name that will determine your victory.

If you're on the backside of an alley, and your name is Rockefeller, there is a problem. But nobody can help you until you know the significance of your name. At the moment you understand your name, you can have nasty, stinky trash all over you, but when you recognize your name is Rockefeller, you are going to come walking up in somebody's place with the authority that emanates from your voice because of what you know now, and they will get you some clean clothes. They will take you over to the Ritz Carlton because you understand who you are.

Even though you still smell, even though every bill you have is still unpaid, your name is righteous, and you are a possessor of heaven and earth. Your name is "More than a Conqueror." Your name is "Inheritor." As soon as you recognize who you are, it doesn't matter what your present circumstances are, they are subject to change.

They will take a back seat.

They will begin to listen to you.

All you have to do is know who you are and they will step back and say, "Oops, I'm sorry. Forgive me for trying to step on top of you."

Know your name. When your name is "*Healed*," what sickness can damn you? When your name is "*Top*," what would you ever be doing swimming around the bottom?

Chapter Thirteen: The Power of an Heir

In many third world nations, when a woman loses her mate, she loses her personhood because there is no man to name her. And in like manner, if you are the oldest son in a family of ten kids, others recognize you not by your given name, but by your family name. If your family's name is nothing, you in essence are nothing.

It works the same way in many of those nations regarding marriage. A person's wealth is determined primarily by their name. When a marriage is to take place, the surname of one family and the surname of another family come together. The fathers in those families come together with the mothers and decide the marriage. They sit for hours talking to each other about the son and the daughter. The children do not talk because if there cannot be a connection of the names, the wedding won't matter. They talk until they both agree, "We have someone who would be suitable for our name."

After that, another meeting is scheduled where the parents of both sides are there, at the same table, with the son and the daughter talking. At this point, they never discuss if they will be together. That has already been established when the father said, "It will work." The father knows what is inherent in the name.

KNOW YOUR NAME; KNOW YOUR FATHER

You have a spiritual name and a spiritual heritage. You are from the Jehovah clan, which means the self-existent One, the all-powerful One. There are parts of your name that you may not know much about, but you need to learn all of the parts of your name.

Learn about the *Adonai* portion of your name that talks about the almightiness of your name.

Learn about the *Shaddai* portion of your name, which means you can never go hungry without Him taking care of you and being your sustenance.

Learn about the *Raphah* portion of your name, which means there isn't a sickness alive that He hasn't taken care of in Christ Jesus.

Learn about the *Jirah* portion of your name, which means He is your Provider.

Learn about the *Shammah* portion of your name, which means you'll never be left by yourself. He's always going to be a very present help in times in trouble.

Learn about the *Shalom* portion of your name, so in times when you could be worried, He's going to bring you peace.

All of those names are part of your heirship!

The heir, as long as he is a child, differeth nothing from a servant, though he be lord of all; But is under tutors and governors until the time appointed of the father. Even so we, when we were children, were in bondage under the elements of the world: But when the fulness of the time was come, God sent forth his Son, made of a woman, made under the law, To redeem them that were under the law, that we might receive the adoption of sons. And because ye are sons, God hath sent forth the Spirit of his Son into your hearts, crying, Abba, Father.

The Greek language says, "My Father, my very own Father." One of the ways you indicate that someone is your father is when you take on their name.

Chapter Thirteen: The Power of an Heir

Wherefore thou art no more a servant, but a son.

You may proclaim, "I am a servant of the Lord."

No, you are not!

"But Bishop, I thought you said we're supposed to serve."

That's absolutely right. You can serve without being a servant. God does not want you competing for a position, for placement, because you are not a servant. A servant has to competitively try to gain a place. But when you know you're a son, you know you have an eternal place.

Wherefore thou art no more a servant, but a son; and if a son, then an heir of God through Christ.

The next verse seems out of context, as though it does not make much sense. He says,

Howbeit then, when ye knew not God, ye did service unto them which by nature are no gods. But now, after that ye have known God, or rather are known of God, how turn ye again to the weak and beggarly elements, whereunto ye desire again to be in bondage? Ye observe days, and months, and times, and years. I am afraid of you, lest I have bestowed upon you labour in vain.

Let me clarify this statement. He is essentially saying, "You are no longer a bond-servant. You no longer need to decide whether God loves you. God loves you, and it has nothing to do with whether you prayed today, or if you did five things right and three things wrong. Being an heir has nothing to do with your actions."

Even though you are an heir, you are not a servant.

You are not a servant. A servant works for his pay; an heir is going to receive, period.

A servant must do something to receive something. An heir will receive just because he woke up in the morning.

Your Works Won't Cut It

When I write about being *kept by the power*, you must understand that you will never work yourself into being kept.

Nothing you can do through works will make God keep you.

"I was praising Him today, so I know He's going to keep me."

"I woke up this morning with my mind stayed on Him. I know He's going to keep me."

No, He's going to keep you because you are born of Him. Because you are saved, because you wear His Name. And that has nothing to do with anything you could ever do in Him. So, the apostle is essentially telling the Galatians, "You are heirs, so why would you go back to counting days, counting times, trying to observe this, trying to observe that?"

You would be surprised how many of God's people are waiting for lightning to come out of the sky because they didn't have a good day. They think He's ready to judge them because they didn't dot the "i's" or cross the "t's".

Chapter Thirteen: The Power of an Heir

Servants operate by an moment-by-moment evalua-evaluative process; heirs function by name and position.

Once we get a hold of the fact that we are heirs, and that heirship has nothing to do with activity, it has nothing to do with our track record, we are on our way to being *kept by the power*.

"Bishop, does that mean we have a license to sin?"

Absolutely not!

Once you know you're an heir, you want to do right and stay right! You want to honor Him whose name you own.

It is a matter of honor.

If your name is Rockefeller, you want to act like one. Whatever your name is, you begin to walk in that direction, to flow in that area. The Patriarchs of old understood that. They understood, "I don't just want to grow up and have a family. No, I want someone to have my name. I want my name out there because just as certain as someone has my name, he has everything I've got."

When you own His name, you own everything He owns.

We used to sing this old song, "My Father is rich in houses and land. He holds the world in the power of His hand. Rubies and diamonds, silver and gold, I am a child of the King wherever I go."

It would have been great if we had understood then the meaning of that song, and believed the words. If you are a child of the King, you do not need to try to get God's blessings.

When you know you are an heir, the whole spirit down inside of you cries out, "My Father, my Father, my very own Father. I don't want to say anything, I don't want to do anything, I don't want to go in any direction that will not be pleasing to You. Because You are my Papa. I just love you because You're Daddy. That's all that matters. I love You."

You Are NOT Secondary!

For so long we have tried to say we are adopted into the things of God. We have called ourselves secondary sons, secondary daughters. The Bible says,

> *He is not a Jew who is one outwardly, but he is a Jew which is one inwardly.*

In other words, no one can insinuate that you are secondary. A Christian is not a secondary Jew. You and I are as much Jews as any Jew is. You are a Jew because you belong to the family of God.

He engrafted you. He put your branch on the same tree, not a secondary tree. Abraham was engrafted as a Jew, just as you are.

You are begotten.

When someone throws the stereotype to you and says, "Man, it seems like the Jewish people are always coming into money," you reply, "Yeah, I know. We always are."

Steven Silbiger chronicled some startling facts in his landmark book *The Jewish Phenomenon: Seven Keys to the Enduring Wealth of a People*. He identifies linking factors as to why he believes the Jewish people are the most wealthy people on earth. I can condense all seven keys down to one: because *we* Jews have a promise! The Lord Jesus has made me a part of Abraham's lineage!

And if ye be Christ's, then are ye Abraham's seed, And heirs according to the promise.
(Galatians 3:29)

According to Mr. Silbiger, the Jewish-American population, though only making up 2 percent of the U.S. population, possesses 50 percent of the wealth. Now, you can spend your time being stuck in your ethnic prison if you want to, but as for me, I am an engrafted Jew, and we own over 50 percent of the wealth!

- You have a promise.
- You have a savior.
- You have an inheritance.

You are a joint heir. Whatever the first heir got, the second heir is going to get too.

You are kept by the power because you are an heir and the wealth is yours. You occupy. You drive out all previous tenants from your possessions. You seize, take, and inherit. You bring to poverty all those who try to stand in your way to keep you from your possessions.

You get what Jesus gets.

You are not a second-class citizen.

You have a promise, a bloodline to possess, to overtake and subdue all.

BIOGRAPHICAL INFORMATION

Bishop Allen B. Coleman is the founder and senior pastor of Voice of Joy Ministries, International in Jacksonville, Florida, and the Presiding Bishop of the International Fellowship of Covenant Churches and Ministries. He is internationally known and regarded as one of the "cutting edge" speakers of our time. The very unique, yet straightforward approach to Bishop Coleman's ministry has allowed him to transcend global barriers with a message of total healing and restoration. His passion for church government and spiritual order has made him a widely respected conference speaker, lecturer, and mentor. Bishop Coleman is a true "Leader of Leaders" and is a dedicated spiritual Father to many devoted sons and daughters.